Denby & District
in the First and
Second World Wars

Dedication

For my Mum, Carol, with love.

Denby & District in the First and Second World Wars

Their Ultimate Sacrifice

Chris Heath

Pen & Sword
MILITARY

First published in Great Britain in 2022 by
Pen & Sword Military
An imprint of
Pen & Sword Books Ltd
Yorkshire – Philadelphia

ISBN 978 1 39909 963 9

A CIP catalogue record for this book is
available from the British Library.

Any errors or omissions are entirely the fault of the author. While every effort has been
made to trace the copyright owners of the illustrations in this book the author wishes to
apologise to anyone who has not been acknowledged. If an error has
occurred, this will be corrected in any subsequent reprint of this work.

Typeset by Mac Style
Printed and bound in the UK by CPI Group (UK) Ltd,
Croydon, CR0 4YY.

Pen & Sword Books Limited incorporates the imprints of Atlas,
Archaeology, Aviation, Discovery, Family History, Fiction, History,
Maritime, Military, Military Classics, Politics, Select, Transport,
True Crime, Air World, Frontline Publishing, Leo Cooper, Remember
When, Seaforth Publishing, The Praetorian Press, Wharncliffe
Local History, Wharncliffe Transport, Wharncliffe True Crime
and White Owl.

For a complete list of Pen & Sword titles please contact

PEN & SWORD BOOKS LIMITED
47 Church Street, Barnsley, South Yorkshire, S70 2AS, England
E-mail: enquiries@pen-and-sword.co.uk
Website: www.pen-and-sword.co.uk

Or

PEN AND SWORD BOOKS
1950 Lawrence Rd, Havertown, PA 19083, USA
E-mail: Uspen-and-sword@casematepublishers.com
Website: www.penandswordbooks.com

Contents

Acknowledgements

Margaret Stansfield, Sandy Hanson, Alison Brook, Christine Stockwell, Becky Slater, Barbara Town, Erica Wainwright, Bob Skrzeczkowski, Jane Raistrick, Diane Brown, Roz Dilly, Barry Lockwood, Terry Lockwood.

Introduction

'There died that day … the finest flower of French chivalry.'

The Battle of Poitiers, 1356.

World history has been dominated by battles and wars, every generation has experienced them. British history is no different. These islands were invaded and conquered by the Romans, after their withdrawal the Irish, Picts, Saxons, Angles and Jutes fought for land and power with the indigenous Britons. Viking raids followed leading to a partial conquest, and then total conquest was achieved by the Normans. Internal strife and foreign conquest followed, wars on land and at sea with the French and Spanish and eventually an all out Civil War changing the country forever. Colonial wars were fought abroad as the British Empire expanded, in America, India and Africa, and more wars with the French Empire during Napoleonic times. Further strife with the Boer and Crimean Wars followed but as the twentieth century began, no one knew or had ever experienced the scale of loss that was to come in the shape of the First World War.

Around 65 million troops fought around the world, 5 million were British.

8½ million troops were killed including 750,000 British servicemen.

21 million were wounded including 1½ million British troops.

An estimated 2 million soldiers, sailors and airmen died from disease, malnutrition and other causes.

An estimated 13 million civilians were also killed.

The flower of British chivalry and youth were cut down in such numbers that they would have staggered those who fought at Poitiers. The War to end all Wars …

Disputes largely left unsettled at the end of the First World War gradually rankled and led to the unthinkable; a Second World War was to follow after a twenty-year hiatus, this was to become the deadliest military conflict in history.

72½ million people died as a result of the war.

24 million soldiers, sailors and airmen were killed in action.

Over 20 million people died as a result of disease and famine.

34 million civilians perished during the war.

6 million Jews were persecuted and lost their lives.

These conflicts impacted on every community in Britain and the sons of the Parish of Denby played their part as did their neighbours in Denby Dale, Skelmanthorpe, Penistone and indeed every hamlet, village, town and city up and down the country. Mothers, wives, lovers, sons and daughters were left to mourn the passing of those who never returned home having paid the ultimate sacrifice. This is not to say that many of those in the conflict did not make it back, the local war memorials record only the dead. Large numbers of veterans joined the local branches of the Royal British Legion; a glance at the records from Denby Dale shows over 200 members for 1946. Many of these told stories of great courage and comradeship; others never spoke of their experiences.

The fallen of Denby were, in most part, the sons of farmers and weavers, blacksmiths, carpenters and butchers. Ordinary men, in or around their early twenties, at the beginning of their careers, some newly married, many single with sweethearts, optimistic about their potential in life as people of this age generally are. They joined the armies of Britain because they believed that the cause was just, unaware of the horrors that awaited them. Information about them varies greatly, for some we know the circumstances of their death, for others, their death is about all we know. Their backgrounds are covered in as much detail as possible in order to know where they came from and what made them who they were. This is an attempt to make them more than words carved on to a family grave in the local churchyard or on war memorials, and to honour them for giving their lives so that ours could be lived to the full in more peaceful times.

I have omitted previously published details regarding both world wars in order to avoid repetition. The story of the foundation and operations of the Denby Dale branch of the British Legion, the war stories of John Gaunt, Leslie Shaw and Joe Price, the story of the two Denby Dale women who joined the Land Army and the conversion of the Victoria Memorial Hall in Denby Dale to a military hospital can all be found in previous volumes, along with much more.

It should be noted that some individuals are remembered on more than one monument in more than one place. In the case of the Birdsedge soldiers during the First World War the names of some of the fallen appear on the Denby Dale war memorial as well as on the Birdsedge Village Hall memorial. For no other reason than I researched the Denby Dale War memorial first, their names are recorded in that section. There are also instances of siblings joining up to fight and I have tended to record these together rather than repeat their family history.

I must also acknowledge the work of the late Margaret Stansfield whose book, *Huddersfield's Roll of Honour* (2014), is an excellent starting place for any historian with an interest in the district's First World War history. This, coupled with the Ancestry and Find My Past websites, enables at least a paragraph or two to be compiled. Due to the fact that the storage facility housing First World War service records was hit by a German bombing raid in the Second World War only forty per cent of these documents have survived into the twenty-first century, often referred to as 'the burnt series', much detail has been lost. It must also be said that due to data protection laws, the records of servicemen and women who served after 1920 (including the Second World War) are not readily accessible yet. I have included very brief details of two of my own family members in the final appendix, but I do not know their service histories and sadly there is no one left to ask now. Only the passage of time will see these records become available and it will be for future historians to update their stories.

This book has been researched and written during a national lockdown due to the Covid–19 pandemic. This has meant that the usual channels of investigation have been impossible to follow, yet the results due to my own archive and that miracle of our age, the internet, have seen largely positive results. I would like to believe that much more evidence has survived from the two world wars in terms of memory and photographs in private collections and sincerely hope that individuals will come forward to enhance any future reprint of this work. There were also people I have researched whose stories are not included due to a paucity of information. For example, I knew the late Jim Barber of Upper Denby, former publican and someone I called a friend, who aided and abetted my research for previous books. I can berate myself as long as I like for not asking him about his war service as he is sadly no longer with us. Records will eventually be released allowing us to discover more, but a person's absence from these pages is no reflection on their accomplishments and is, almost, purely due to the Data Protection Act. Oh to be able to go back to when I first began asking questions. Speaking of the current pandemic, as I write more than four million people worldwide have tragically died throughout its duration. Millions more have suffered with its symptoms and countless masses have self-isolated, missing family and friends, international travel is all but halted, any plans that were made are all on hold, holidays are nothing but memories – and even Hitler didn't shut the pubs. Yet. The same spirit that brought our ancestors through the two worst conflicts in human history still survives. Perhaps, when things return to normal, or as normal as can be, we will all have had time for thought and reflection and we will all embrace the present and the future with a zeal hitherto unknown and care about the past with a passion for what our forebears endured on our behalf.

Finally, if there are readers of this book with details or photographs of any individuals mentioned herein that would add to any potential reprint of this work then I would be delighted to hear from them at denbyfallen@gmail.com.

Historical Note 1: A number of the soldiers featured in this book are listed as of the Parish of Fulstone. Historically Fulstone was a township in the Parish of Kirkburton, which included New Mill and Scholes, which, together with six other townships, formed the Graveship of Holme. It stretched as far as Jackson Bridge in the west to Lane Head, Shepley in the east and as far south as Broadstone Reservoir. At its eastern side it followed the Dearne Dike Road just to the west of Birdsedge, which is why a number of soldiers can be found residing at Fulstone when in fact they were living in the eastern part of Fulstone Parish but their nearest village was Birdsedge, hence their commemoration on the village war memorial.

Historical Note 2: Within the pages of this book I have had cause to mention Denby Delf which can also be spelt Delph. I have opted to use the former spelling which is an old English word for a stone or clay quarry. The Delph spelling has Scottish roots, though the two were interchangeable in old records and both are similarly still in use today.

For the Fallen

With proud thanksgiving, a mother for her children,
England mourns for her dead across the sea.
Flesh of her flesh they were, spirit of her spirit,
Fallen in the cause of the free.

Solemn the drums thrill; Death august and royal
Sings sorrow up into immortal spheres,
There is music in the midst of desolation
And a glory that shines upon our tears.

They went with songs to the battle, they were young,
Straight of limb, true of eye, steady and aglow.
They were staunch to the end against odds uncounted;
They fell with their faces to the foe.

They shall grow not old, as we that are left grow old:
Age shall not weary them, nor the years condemn.
At the going down of the sun and in the morning
We will remember them.

They mingle not with their laughing comrades again;
They sit no more at familiar tables of home;
They have no lot in our labour of the day-time;
They sleep beyond England's foam.

But where our desires are and our hopes profound,
Felt as a well-spring that is hidden from sight,
To the innermost heart of their own land they are known
As the stars are known to the Night;

As the stars that shall be bright when we are dust,
Moving in marches upon the heavenly plain;
As the stars that are starry in the time of our darkness,
To the end, to the end, they remain.

By Laurence Binyon

The Fallen of Upper Denby Parish

First World War

Private Charles Kilner Barraclough

Born – Upper Denby, 18 May 1883.
Died – Passchendaele, 8 October 1917.
Regimental No.103293.

Charles Kilner Barraclough was born into an old Denby family of farmers, butchers and blacksmiths. The family as we currently have it begins with James Barraclough, also written Barrowclough (1712–1782), who was born at Shepley and married Barbara Berry (1708–1781). They had a son, James (1730–1813) who married Ann Haigh and who baptised his children at Upper Denby. Twelve of them in fact, which leads to two family trees in the village. James's occupation is currently unknown but the fact he rented land off the Lord of the Manor, George Savile, through the latter end of the eighteenth century is suggestive of farming. For instance, in 1791 he paid 6s 4d for his home and land and in 1796, approaching older age, he had reduced his operations to 1s 9d, which may be an acknowledgement of his age. His offspring remained in Lower Denby but it is through his fifth child, Isaac (1764–1824) that we follow the descent. Isaac died before the census returns made a debut, but his family afterwards was firmly associated with Exley Gate at Lower Denby so without further evidence we might assume farming was a feature of his life. He married Hannah Baum and can be found in the Staincross registers of alehouse keepers in 1803:

1803 Licensed alehouse keepers at Denby:

William Kilner, Isaac Barraclough, Jonathan Graham, Joseph Wood, Jonathan Gaunt, Edward Horn all charged at £10.

His son, Isaac (1799–1879) lived at Dry Hill, Lower Denby, and worked as a livestock farmer of 26 acres and was also, naturally, a butcher. He married Ellen Armitage and had at least ten children, including John (1845–1919). Isaac hadn't altered his circumstances by 1861, he still farmed 26 acres, but by 1871 he had increased his holdings to 34 acres, still at Dryhill, and his daughter, Mary, was included in the census returns of that year as a 30-year-old dairy maid. Isaac died in 1879 but it is through his son, John (1845–1919) we follow the descent. John married Maria Hanwell, the daughter of Upper Denby publican, John Hanwell

(The New Inn) and wasn't always as well behaved as he should have been. A record from March 1879 shows that he was imprisoned at HMP Wakefield for one month, for assaulting his wife. He was recorded as a farmer/butcher. He was released in April and according to his prison record was 5ft 8in tall with brown hair, 34 years old and no previous convictions. Thankfully, there were no further lapses – lesson learned. Prior to this, John had been recorded in the 1871 census returns as a master butcher at Exley gate, but by 1881 he had become a labourer at an iron works. In 1891 he was a weighman at a steel works and by 1911 had moved from Exley Gate to Upper Denby, where he can be found living with just his daughter, Elizabeth, aged 31.

John and Maria had at least eight children. The eldest son, Lewis married twice, first to Ruth Crossley at Denby in 1902, then to Charlotte Hinchliffe in 1908. In 1911 the couple were living at Exley Gate with Charlotte's father when Lewis was recorded as an engine cleaner at a steelworks. The second son, Ernest, was a woollen weaver, he married Ann Harrison and moved to Back lane, Shelley, where he had a family.

Upper Denby Church circa 1900.

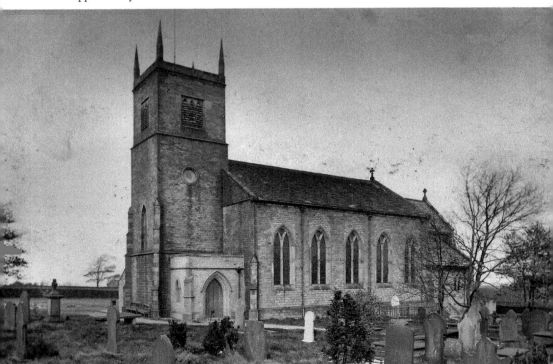

The youngest son, Charles Kilner Barraclough was born 18 May 1883, and after attending Denby National School he married Florence Wrigley at St Peters Church, Huddersfield in 1910. After the marriage they removed to Castleford Road, Normanton, Wakefield, where Charles became a superintendent of assurance, a big step on from 1901 when he was recorded in Denby as unemployed. Charles was also later noted to be employed as a travelling representative by G.H. Inman, Mineral Water Manufacturer, while living at Marsh, Huddersfield. While here he became a committee member of March Conservative Club and a member of the Manchester Order of Oddfellows and attended Holy Trinity Church, Huddersfield. Charles and Florence also had a son in 1911, Ronald Stuart.

Charles Kilner Barraclough enlisted for the war at Huddersfield as a Private in the 204th Machine Gun Corps and was killed in action at Passchendaele on 8 October 1917. He has no known grave but is commemorated on the Tyne Cot Memorial to the Missing, Belgium.

All-in-One Tree of Joseph Barraclough

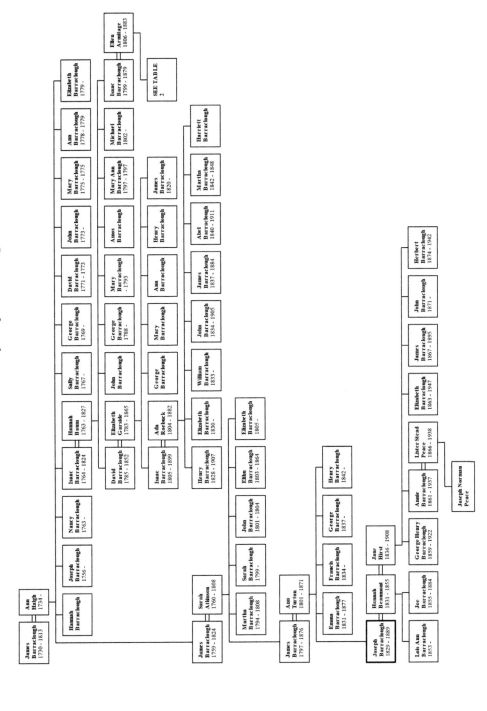

All-in-One Tree of Charles Kilner Barraclough

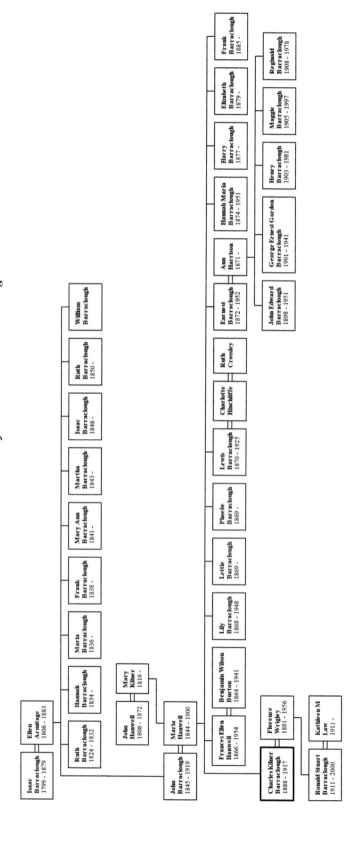

Private Gladstone Beever

Born – Upper Denby, July 1896.
Died – France/Flanders, 15 September 1916.
Regimental No. 24050.

Gladstone Beever was born into a family that had deep roots in the Denby and Gunthwaite area. His great-grandfather, Jonas Beever was born in about 1791, lived at Nether Denby and was an agricultural labourer. He married Alice Hawksworth (1792–1849) who was a member of the Gunthwaite and Cawthorne land-owning family and one time rivals of the Bosville Lords of the manor of Gunthwaite. The Hawksworths' interest in land and property was much diluted by the time of this marriage but their roots in the area go back to pre-Tudor times.

Jonas and Alice had at least four children of whom William (1834–1891) was the third, he married Esther Wood and had eleven children, all at Denby. William spent much of his life working as a labourer, probably in agriculture as the two main occupations in and around his home were farming and textiles. His eldest son, George (1856–1935) found work as a quarryman driver and labourer and his second son, Hugh (1862–1942) became a labourer at the steel works by 1891. Hugh later followed his elder brother and became a stone dresser and quarryman in both 1901 and 1911. He married Hannah Williams and had nine children; again, all at Denby, and Gladstone was the eldest of these being born in 1897. By 1939 Hugh was living at Low Fold, a widower and described as incapacitated, he died in 1942.

We can find Gladstone in the 1911 census returns working 'carrying off pipes' for one of the local sanitary pipe manufacturers, probably either Naylor's or Kitson's works in Denby Dale. Later he worked for the Denby Dale weaving company Z Hinchliffe & Sons. He joined up for the war effort with the 2nd Battalion York and Lancaster Regiment and sailed to France in June 1916. He was killed in action very shortly after on 15 September 1916. He has no known grave but is remembered on the Thiepval Memorial to the Missing in France.

All-in-One Tree of Gladstone Beever

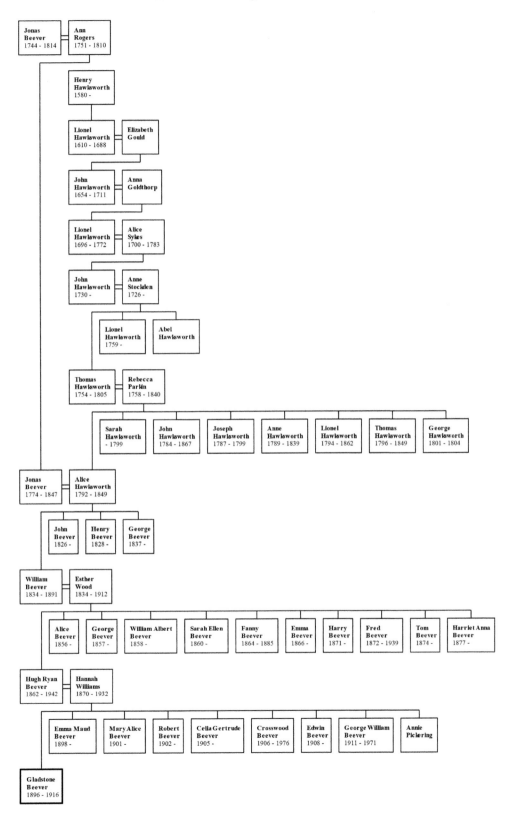

Private Charles Ralph Douglas Bell

Born – Maitland, New South Wales, Australia, December 1896.
Died – Amiens, Somme, France, 6 July 1918.
Regimental No. 4531

Our story for this individual begins in Lincolnshire with Charles John Bell who was born around 1760. His son, William was born in Louth in 1784 and married Rebecca Park and they had a son, Charles (1820–1900), who is recorded as a gamekeeper in the 1851 and 1861 census returns. Living in Hainston, Lincolnshire, Charles married Jane Chapman and had at least five children, all in Lincolnshire at villages such as Hainton, Withern and Benniworth. The fourth of these, Charles Parr Bell (1849–1900), immigrated to New Zealand at some point between 1861 and 1881 where he met and married his wife, Alice Dorothy Sophia Sercombe, and had a son, Arthur George Henry Bell, in 1888. The second of Charles and Jane Bell's children, Henry Baker Bell (born 1844) married Mary Elizabeth Borman and had two sons, Charles John (1866–1900) and Frederick Bell. Whether encouraged by the success of his Uncle Charles in New Zealand, Charles John also immigrated but this time to Sydney, Australia on 17 May 1882. Here he met and married his wife, Pauline Weingardner at Bathurst, New South Wales in 1889 with whom he had three sons, including the youngest Charles Ralph Douglas Bell born in December 1896.

Charles Ralph Douglas Bell was 18 years old when he first enlisted in the Australian army in 1915. He was described as a farm labourer on 12 May 1915 when he joined the 18th Battalion, 1st Reinforcements and embarked on the ship HMAT A32 *Themistocles* at Sydney. At some point within the next year Charles had returned home on leave, but on 23 April 1916 he was once again sailing to war. This time he became a part of the 6th Infantry Division which was itself a part of the 23rd Infantry Battalion, 11th Reinforcements. This time he was described more briefly as a labourer when he boarded the ship RMS *Malwa*. On both occasions his mother, Pauline, was listed as next of kin as Charles's father had passed away prematurely in 1900 aged only 34. The family home address was 380 Crown Street, Sunnyhills, New South Wales. We will re-examine this part of Charles's military career in more depth a little later.

At some point during the next year we know that Charles landed in England, and here I might make a confession. I had given up on trying to track down young Charles as I could not find any record of his presence in Upper Denby, the nearby villages, West Yorkshire or even the British Isles. I was in the process of going back through my collection of Penistone Almanacs looking for other individuals when I came, quite by chance (and very luckily) to the Baptisms, Marriages and Funerals section in the 1918 edition. In the Upper Denby marriage list the following brief line re-ignited the story:

1917. April 1st. Charles Ralph Douglas Bell, Australia married Maude Minna Burley of Denby.

But who was Maude Minna Burley? It is to Bradfield we must travel to unravel her origins. Josh Burley can be found living here in the late eighteenth century. His son, John (1797–1875) moved on to Hoylandswaine where he worked as a farmer of thirty acres at Hill Top. He married Eliza Crossland and had at least five children. Charles Burley (1854–1925) was the youngest and was also a farmer, though he worked out of High Royd in Hoylandswaine. He married Sarah Jane Apperley (originally from Gloucestershire) and had six children all born at the farm and Maude Minna (1886–1963) was the couple's second daughter. Interestingly by 1901 Charles Burley was noted to be working as an above ground colliery labourer. We will return to Maude's younger brother, John who joined the RAF later in this book.

In 1911 Maude, aged 25, can be found living and working as a general domestic servant for Herbert and Harriet Thompson Musgrave and their family at Burley in Wharfedale. Herbert was a hydraulic engineer which goes a little way to explain this family's affluence. The rest of the story we can only guess at. Evidently Maud returned to the Hoylandswaine vicinity and perhaps even found work at Upper Denby. At some point, one presumes, in 1916, Charles Ralph Godfrey Bell and Maude Burley met and had long enough to fall in love and decide to get married. It is currently impossible to say why Charles was at Denby at all, but as we have seen they did marry on All Fools Day 1917 (also Easter Monday) – perhaps they should have known. The wedding was conducted by Denby Vicar, Romeo Edwin Taglis, and witnessed by Harry Thorpe and Maude's sister, Mira Evelyn Burley. Maude was noted to be living at High Flatts; Charles was stationed at Fovant army camp, around nine miles west of Salisbury in Wiltshire. One of a number of camps which sprang up in and around Salisbury Plain it was temporary home to 20,000 men in prefabricated wooden huts, clad in corrugated iron, including the roofs, each hut contained a central wood-burning stove and housed about thirty men to each unit. The camp was largely used for training exercises and had a hospital which grew in size due to the numbers of casualties reporting back from the trenches. An increased Australian presence took place from March 1917 as their forces grew and, of course, this would have included Charles.

Presumably after the wedding Charles and Maude returned to her home at High Flatts – this at least explains why his name is a part of the list of the fallen of Denby as he would have returned here when the war was over. It would be interesting to speculate on the reaction of Maude's parents to what appears to be a whirlwind romance ending in a wartime marriage to a man eleven years her junior, but she was now 31 years old, of independent means and would have been confident of her decision. For Charles, love and marriage had to be put aside as he still had a war to fight.

Now that we have a little more information about Charles we can explore a fairly large number of records that have survived him.

His enlistment papers of 1915 give the following description: He was 5ft 3in tall, 10st 7lbs, had a ruddy complexion, brown eyes and dark hair. He had been in the Commonwealth Cadets for three years prior to the war. It was also prior to the war that Charles can be found falling foul of the local Constabulary, perhaps giving us a clue to his temperament:

New South Wales Police Gazette, 9 July 1913.
Darlinghurst.

A warrant, where a summons is disobeyed, has been issued by the Water Police Bench for the arrest of Ralph Charles Douglas Bell, charged with committing a breach of the Defence Act, at Sydney, on 3 May last. Offender is about 17 years old, 5ft 6in high, stout build, dark complexion and hair, large dark eyes; dressed in dark clothes and tweed cap. Complainant, G.H.M King, Area Officer, Area 26A.

His war service begins as follows:

27 April 1915
Depart from Liverpool with the 18th Battalion and then to Egypt on 12 May 1915.

3 August 1915
Transferred from Abassia DBI Hospital to Australia with venereal disease.

4 August 1915
Aboard the *Port Lincoln* en route to Australia via the Suez Canal.

2 September 1915
Disembarked in Australia suffering with gonorrhoea. Transferred to Broadmeadows Isolation Hospital, Victoria.

27 September 1915
Discharged Isolation Hospital, Langwarrin, as fit for duty.

10 February 1916
Declared under the Army Act 72 to be a deserter, the Army Board convened at Broadmeadows on this date. He had been AWOL from 9 October 1915 and his whereabouts were still unknown when the Court met. He was struck off from the Reserve Regiment as punishment.

20 March 1916
Rejoins the 23rd Battalion, 11th Regiment. (No details on his previous misconduct are on this second set of recruitment papers.)

21 March 1916
Embarked at Melbourne on the *Malwa*.

19 April 1916
Disembarked at Suez.

19 November 1916
Embarked on the SS *Onward* for France and was in Etapes on 20 November.

9 December 1916 – 23 June 1917
Active in France in the Rouen area. He was admitted to hospital on 23 June suffering from an old gunshot wound to the thigh.

So it would appear that when Charles and Minna married in April at Upper Denby he had been sent to Fovant Camp for further training or recuperation. He had returned to France, presumably after his agreed leave period had ended, the next record we find is:

9 July 1917
Invalided to England from France on board the HS *Kaylan*, still suffering from the old thigh wound. He was taken to the University War Hospital at Dartford.

10 August 1917
Transferred from University War Hospital to Auxiliary Hospital.

11–25 August 1917
Discharged from Auxiliary Hospital to furlough.

8 October 1917
Overseas training at Perham Downs, on the Eastern edge of Salisbury Plain, Wiltshire.

13 January 1918
Training at Fovant Camp.

14 April 1918
Offence. AWOL from 5 April till 1pm 7 April, forfeit five days pay. (This does make one wonder if a trip to High Flatts had been involved?).

20 May 1918
Proceeded overseas to France with the 5th Training Battalion from Fovant to Folksestone and to Havre.

1 June 1918
Rejoined unit from sick. No new details are posted so this was maybe the old thigh wound causing trouble again.

The next definite record we have of him is that he was badly wounded in action on 4 July 1918. Initially this was reported to be a gunshot wound to the abdomen but later this altered to a stab wound while fighting at close quarters near Amiens, Somme, Picardie. He was taken for treatment to the 47th Casualty Clearing Station, which was at that time near Varennes in North East France. He died of wounds on 6 July and is buried in Crouy British Cemetery aged 21. It is unknown how much time Charles had to spend with his wife. The marriage had lasted all of fifteen months and it is possible the pair never met again after Charles's leave to marry had ended – though his second AWOL offence might suggest otherwise. There is no local evidence of any children.

Charles's effects upon the event of his death were originally meant to have been sent to his mother, but his marriage had been noted by the Military and they were in fact sent to Maude at Millbank Farm, High Flatts on 27 August 1918. They consisted of the following:

1 disc, photos, 1 pipe, 1 small mirror, notebook, whistle, lanyard, photo case, fountain pen, badges, metal pencil holder, 1 (gold?) photo pendant, 1 key, 1 broken gold ring (stones missing), 1 YMCA wallet, 2 wallets, 1 purse, coins, 1 half franc note, 1 50 centime note.

It is probable that Maude moved on to East Anglia. A record dating to 1939 records a Maude M. Bell living on Essex Street in Norwich and recording her birthday as 16 January 1886. We know that our Maude was born in January. She was noted to be undertaking unpaid domestic duties on behalf of her co-occupier, John Burley, a light joiner aged twenty-one months younger than Maude and surely her younger brother – John. Maude later moved back to West Yorkshire, this time to 280 Selby Road, Halton, Leeds. It was at St James Hospital in the city, in 1963, that her death as a widow aged 77 is recorded. Her effects were handled by a solicitor and amounted to £783 1s.

All-in-One Tree of Charles Ralph Douglas Bell

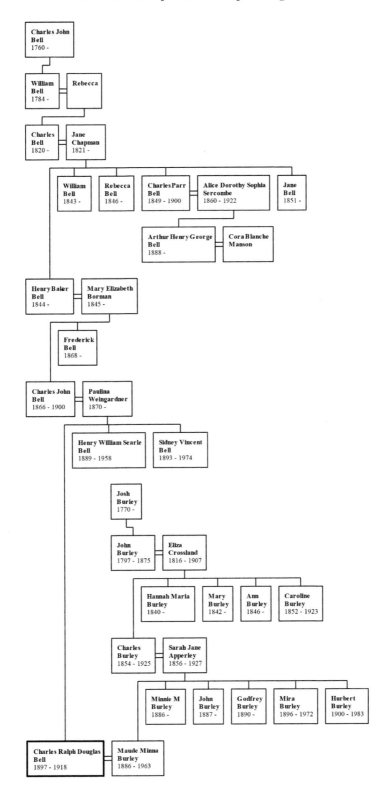

Lance Corporal George Clement Boothroyd

Born – Upper Denby 1888.
Died – France/Flanders, 9 February 1917.
Regimental No. 28792.

George Clement Boothroyd came from a long established line of tailors. His great-grandfather, Benjamin (1786–1830) was born at Almondbury but lived for a while at High Flatts. He married Hannah Tyas and at least three of their children became tailors (and probably some of the others as well). The eldest, Richard (1824–1901) was born in Denby and married Martha Wright, Martha died soon after the death of the couple's fourth child John (1859–1935), and it was not practical for Richard to bring up his own children at that time. Two of them, Clement and the above named John, were sent to live with their uncle Benjamin at Manor Farm in Upper Denby. Benjamin did not let the side down, as well as being a farmer he also operated as a tailor, he can be found here in the 1841 census returns as a tailor, living with his widowed mother. His sister, Elizabeth was a dressmaker, his brother Henry, a tailor and another brother, George was a fancy weaver, items of clothing for this family should not have been a problem. Benjamin also taught his nephew, John to be a tailor; indeed the Boothroyd family became synonymous with the profession in Denby for a number of years. Benjamin's younger brother George, who we noted as fancy weaver above, also went on to become a tailor. He was only around 14 at the time of the 1841 census but by 1861 he was living on Birdsedge Hill with his wife Mary Ann and their young family and operating as a tailor. By 1871 they were living on Peace Row in Birdsedge and he was now a tailor and draper, a natural progression.

Returning to Denby it is of interest to note the 1871 census returns for Benjamin Boothroyd and his brother Henry, living next door to one another:

Henry Boothroyd	Head	48	Master Tailor and Local Methodist Preacher	Denby
Mary Boothroyd	Wife	46		Gunthwaite
Arthur Boothroyd	Son	21	Tailor's assistant	Denby
Sabina Boothroyd	Daughter	19	Machinist	Denby

Benjamin Boothroyd	Head	58	Tailor & Farmer of 66 acres	Denby
Sarah Boothroyd	Wife	54		Denby
Mehetabel Boothroyd	Daughter	23		Denby
Manoah Boothroyd	Son	22	Farmer's son	Denby
Clement Boothroyd	Nephew	17		Denby
John Boothroyd	Nephew	13		Denby

Benjamin Boothroyd died in 1879, but by this time his two nephews had come of age and as we have noted, John continued the family tailoring business. He also got married, to Emily Windle of Kirkburton, though there were a number of Windle family members living in Denby at this time. They went to live at Lower Denby where they had six children, George Clement Boothroyd was the fourth born in 1889.

George Clement Boothroyd was working as a stonemason as recorded in the 1911 census returns, when he would have been around 23 years old. Living in such a small community it is very probable he knew another of the fallen of Denby: Keble Thomas Evennett, who also lived at Lower Denby, had married Rosie Thickett and was living with her parents and sister. As Keble was also a tailor and had lodged at Upper Denby near to the Boothroyds at Manor Farm, it is almost a certainty. George joined up with the 2nd Battalion Duke of Wellington's Regiment; he was 27 years old when he enlisted in 1916. He became a Lance Corporal but died of wounds at No. 5 Casualty Clearing Station, France on 9 February 1917 aged 28. He is buried in Bray Military Cemetery, Bray Sur Somme, France.

All-in-One Tree of George Clement Boothroyd

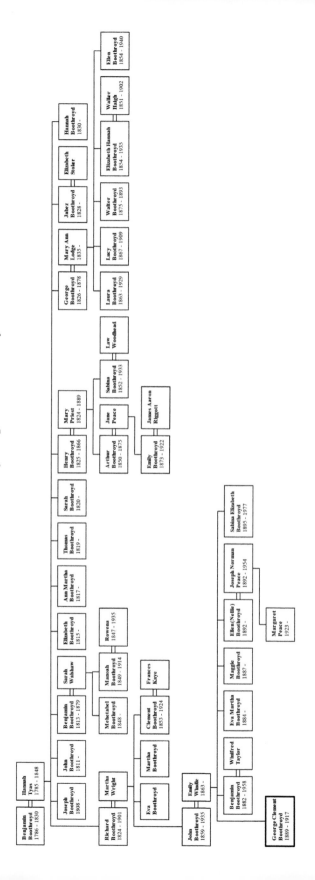

Gunner John Ellis Broadhead

Born – Marsh, Huddersfield 14 May 1874.
Died – Palestine/Egypt 13 October 1918.
Regimental No. 117358.

John Ellis Broadhead was the son of George Broadhead (born 1853) and his wife Elizabeth Ann Lyth. George was born at Jackson Bridge and began his working life as a joiner. In 1871 he was boarding with a family member, David Broadhead, at Fulstone, who was also a joiner and it is likely that George was his apprentice. The census returns show that after his marriage George's first two children, John Ellis and George Henry, were born at Marsh, Huddersfield, though they were baptised at Upper Denby. By the time the couple's third son, Frank, was born in 1885 they had moved to Lower Denby, where George had now taken on a farm as well as continuing with a little joinery on the side. The family were still here in 1911 though the two eldest sons had moved on. Fred, the youngest son, can be found working as a farm hand and John Lyth, a farm servant, also assisted with the day to day running of the farm.

John Ellis Broadhead had married Ellen Ann, daughter of Joseph and Sarah Ann Hudson at Upper Denby in 1899. He was listed to be a farmer at Lower Denby while Ellen was a weaver. They set up home in Wakefield on South Street, largely due to John's employment as a railway

All-in-One Tree of John Ellis Broadhead

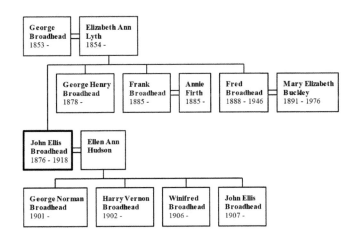

goods master at Wakefield train station. All four of their children were born at Wakefield between 1901 and 1907 and can be found living with their parents on Marsland Street, Wakefield in 1911.

John enlisted with the 394th Siege Battery Royal Garrison Artillery on 25 February 1916 aged 39. He died of malaria in Palestine on 13 October 1918 aged 42 and is buried in Ramleh War Cemetery, Palestine.

Upper Denby Church from Falledge Lane, circa 1900.

Lieutenant Frank Eaden Cook

Born – Lindley, Huddersfield 1891.
Died – France/Flanders 1918.
Regimental No. PS/4669.

Private John (Jack) Eaden Cook

Born – Lindley, Huddersfield 1892.
Died – High Wood, Somme, France 1916.
Regimental No. PS4671.

Above left, Frank Eaden Cook, right John Eaden Cook.

Frank Eaden and John Eaden Cook are our first pair of brothers to take part in the First World War and not to survive till the armistice.

The family originated from Taunton, Somerset, where John Cook was born in 1828. He married Susan Eaden from Cambridge and had at least five children. By 1861 John and Susan were living in Wellington, Somerset, John was described as a linen woollen draper which belies just how well he was doing in business. Also in his household was Mary Selina Jones, working as an assistant milliner (hats), four drapers' assistants, a domestic servant and a groom. What attracted John to move to the North of England is not known, but the huge scale production of textiles may have been the ultimate lure. By 1871 he and his family were residing at Brunswick Place, Huddersfield, where he was now listed as a shoddy manufacturer. Shoddy was the name given to an inferior woollen yarn made by shredding scraps of woollen rags into fibres, grinding them and then mixing them with small amounts of new wool. The object was to manufacture a cheap cloth which could be made into products and clothes. It was also known as Rag-Wool. Rather than have live-in workers John had premises of his own, though he and his family were still looked after by a cook and a housemaid. Further moves followed; in 1881 he was at Fartown and by 1901 and 1911 at Birkby, described as a waste merchant until he retired.

Two of John's sons worked for the business before branching out on their own. Ernest Eaden Cook was noted to be a wool merchant and the eldest, Frederick Lilley Cook can be found working alongside his father in 1881. In 1889 Frederick had married Eleanor Beatrice Wilkinson in Altrincham, Cheshire, and they began a family while living at Lindley, Huddersfield, with Frank Eaden (named after his grandmother) being born in 1891. At this point Frederick was listed as a commercial traveller, but during the next decade his fortunes improved and the family moved out into the countryside. The 1901 census returns record Frederick, Eleanor and their four children living at Middle House, High Flatts, near Upper Denby. Also within their household were Frederick's accountant and a servant Ruth Watts, and Frederick was described as a woollen manufacturer. The 1911 census records Frederick as a wool and woollen waster merchant which more closely follows the trade of his father. They also show that he employed Sarah Burrows, age 17, as a domestic cook and Amy Gell, 21, as a housemaid. Middle House was a very comfortable nine-room house at the secluded hamlet known as Quaker Bottom at High Flatts, the Quaker movement being established here back in the mid-seventeenth century.

By now, Frank Eaden Cook was 20 and worked as a commercial traveller in his father's business, now known as Messrs. Cook, Sons and Company Limited of Huddersfield and Dewsbury. John (known as Jack)

Eaden, just a year younger, was a designer, also in the wool trade for the owner of Birdsedge Mill, Furman Hunt McGrath; he also played amateur football for Thornhill. Both boys had been educated at New College, an independent preparatory school in Harrogate, and would have been well placed to take over and augment their father's business when the time came – but then came the war. Both of them enlisted with the 20th (Public Schools) Battalion of the Royal Fusiliers on 1 September 1914. Frank was appointed a Lance Corporal in October 1914 and then promoted to Corporal in October 1915 before becoming a Sergeant in July 1916. He obtained his commission in November 1916 in the 1/10th Battalion Manchester Regiment and was made a full Lieutenant in April 1918. It was also in 1918 that Frank married Nora Richardson of Fartown.

Both brothers arrived in France on 14 November 1915. On 11 March 1916, Frank was wounded at La Bassee and probably was not with the Battalion in time for their part in the action at High Wood on 20 July. John was there though and was one of the 169 casualties recorded on that day, 114 of which have no known grave. According to Huddersfield historian, Margaret Stansfield, Jack:

> was noticed by his Officer to be wounded and on his way to the field dressing station. He was also seen by a fellow Private further down the line but was never seen again.

John was one of the 114 without a grave, though he is remembered on the Thiepval Memorial to the Missing; he was 24 years old.

Frank was wounded again, at the Somme on 16 August 1917, by a bullet wound through the calf of the left leg and was sent back to England for treatment in Manchester. On 30 August 1918 he was awarded the Military Cross for the part he played in connection with the capture of a village, the citation goes on:

> This officer, minding that the platoon on his left was held up, after reconnoitring the hostile position, successfully pushed on with his platoon, with great gallantry and skill drove the enemy from his position, thus enabling the platoon on his left to gain its objective. Twice he led his platoon forward at critical moments. This initiative and determination greatly assisted towards the success of the operation.
> *London Gazette* 11 January 1919.

He was presented with his medal in the field on 7 October 1918 but only thirteen days later, less than a month before the armistice, Frank was killed in action on 20 October 1918, aged 28. He is buried at Belle Vue British Cemetery, Briastre, France. His medal was sent home to his wife, Nora after his death. In 1919, Nora gave birth to Frank's son, Frank Wilkinson Cook.

Frank and John's younger brother, Alan Evelyn Cook, was also involved in hostilities, though as he was not born until 1899 it was limited. He joined the Royal Air Force on 27 April 1918, No. 137551, thankfully for his parents, he survived those few months and returned home. Frederick and Eleanor Cook left High Flatts, possibly when Frederick retired in 1926. They moved South to Amersham, Buckinghamshire, where Eleanor died in 1933 and Frederick in 1940. Alan Evelyn went on to marry and have two children living at Old Trafford in Manchester before moving to Hawkshurst, Kent, by 1939, he died in 1984 in Milton Keynes. His sister, Margaret Eleanor Cook, never married; after boarding school at The Grange in Buxton she spent time in the USA and Canada during

Frank Eaden Cook. (*Courtesy Birdsdge Village Hall*)

John (Jack) Eaden Cook. (*Courtesy Birdsedge Village Hall*)

Alan Evelyn Cook.

Frederick Lilley and Eleanor Cook.

Middle House, High Flatts.

the 1920s, but eventually finished up in Amersham living with her parents, after their deaths she stayed in the family home until she died in 1947. It is possible that she spent time with her uncle Ernest while in the USA as he had emigrated in 1887 and became a naturalised US citizen in 1894 living at Napa County, California.

Ernest Eaden Cook.

All in one Tree of Frank and John Eaden Cook

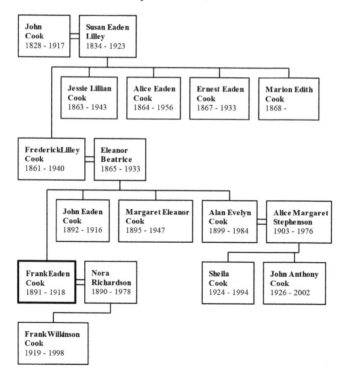

Private Keble Thomas Evennett

Keble Thomas Evennett with his wife Rosie
(Rosetta) outside their home in Lower Denby.

Born – London 17 August 1885.
Died – France 25 February 1918.
Regimental No. 204359

Keble Thomas Evennett was a Londoner, his family residing in Stepney for many years. His grandfather, John Evennett (born 1833), a bricklayer, married Emily Hayward and had at least six children in Stepney, the third of whom was Thomas (1859–1923). Thomas was described as a general labourer in the census returns and lived at Mile End, Old Town, Stepney. He married Mary Jane Chamberlain and had two children, Edwin Francis (1884–1964) and Keble Thomas (1885–1918). These were very interesting times to be living at this location in London, in 1888 a spate of gruesome serial killings began very nearby which stumped the police and still cause widespread debate to this day, we are, of course, talking about Jack the Ripper.

It is unknown as to why Keble abandoned Stepney for Upper Denby, though there may be a few clues as we shall shortly see. In the 1891 census returns for Denby we find him boarding at the home of Lister Stead and Annie Peace along with their son, Joseph Norman, and a fellow boarder, James Aaron Riggott. Lister Peace was a relative of the Denby Dale mill-owning Peace family, but he himself was a tailor; James Riggott was also a tailor, Keble was a tailor's apprentice.

While at Denby, Keble had met Rosetta Thickett, known as Rosie, and in 1908 they were married at Upper Denby church, the wedding being witnessed by Rosie's sister Annie and Joe Willie Heath, a friend of Keble and relative of Lister Peace. This is where the slightly odd evidence comes in to play. The details in the parish register state that Keble's father was dead, when in fact he did not die until 1923. Keble also states that his father was a cook, but in the available evidence, Thomas Evennett was only ever described as a labourer. Further evidence of a denial of Stepney came about in the census returns of 1901 when Keble was described as of the 'UK' in the where born column. It is possible that he left Stepney after a quarrel of some sort, he certainly seems to have severed all ties with his relatives but as only oral evidence of this would survive and at this length of time afterwards we may never know.

Rosetta Thickett was born in Denby in 1878, her father George (1849–1907) was a Shepley man though his father, Joseph (born 1819) was born at Upper Denby. George was a platelayer on the railways, he married Emma Prestidge and had two daughters, the other being Annie, who was 7 years older than Rosie. Annie can be found in 1901 working as a worsted weaver; Rosie, aged 16, was a doffer in a worsted yarn factory. A doffer was someone who removed ('doffs') bobbins, pirns or spindles holding spun fibre such as cotton or wool from a spinning frame and replaced them with empty ones. Historically, spinners, doffers, and sweepers each had separate tasks that were required in the manufacture of spun textiles. From the early days of the industrial revolution, this work, which requires speed and dexterity rather than strength, was often done by children or young women.

Lister Stead Peace.

Lister Stead Peace in his garden on Northgate, Upper Denby.

Keble Thomas Evennett's memorial inscription on the Thickett grave in Upper Denby churchyard.

Keble and Rosie lived at Lower Denby after their marriage, at this time Keble was working as a tailor in his own right. In fact it would appear that after their marriage they simply carried on with their previous arrangements, living with Rosie's parents and sister who had been here since at least 1901. It is also highly likely that Keble knew another of those from Denby to fall in battle, George Clement Boothroyd, who came from a long line of tailors and who also lived at Lower Denby.

In about 1915, Keble enlisted as a Private with the 2/4th Duke of Wellington's Regiment. We know he was in France by 1917 and saw action, but conditions in the trenches were unsanitary and he died of pneumonia at Number 42 Casualty Clearing Station on 25 February 1918, aged 32. He is buried at Aubigny Communal Cemetery Extension in France.

George Thickett died in 1907, his daughter Annie in 1937, and his wife, Emma, in 1944 (aged 96), all were buried at Denby church, the memorial stone records them and Rosie who is buried with them when she died in 1956 aged 69, Keble Thomas Evennett's name is also on the stone.

In an interesting aside, Keble's elder brother also became a private during the Great War. He had married Florence Baker and had a family of at least six children, all born in West Ham. He became a part of the Labour Corps and wasn't demobbed until 18 February 1919 at Folkestone. His discharge papers stated that he was physically unfit due to ulcerated legs, though he must have recovered sufficiently as he was working as a dock labourer in 1939.

All-in-One Tree of Keble Thomas Evennett

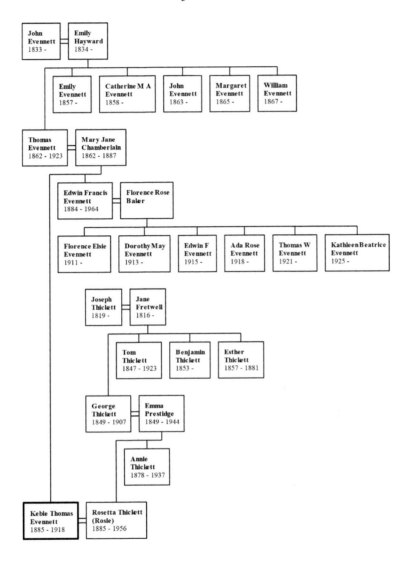

Private Fred Firth

Born – Upper Denby 4 October 1894.
Died – France 8 October 1915.
Regimental No. 13240.

Fred Firth's origins begin in Emley with John Firth, who was born in about 1720 and married Martha Brown in the village. They had a son, John, who was born in Cumberworth in 1740, though he married an Emley girl, Martha Crossley (1739–1777). Their son, Jonathan (1772–1853), was born at Cumberworth and he married Elizabeth Barraclough at Penistone, the couple then lived at Upper Denby and went on to produce ten children. The eldest son, another John (1802–1862), was noted to be a farmer in the village, but in the 1851 and 1861 census returns he is also recorded as an Innkeeper, and from other sources we know he was the landlord of the Star Inn at Upper Denby from at least 1838 to 1861, possibly until his death only a year later. He married Elizabeth Marsden and had a family of at least twelve children including Benjamin (1850–1922). Benjamin, a mechanical engineer, married Eliza Barraclough, a second inter-marriage within three generations for the Firth and Barraclough families, and had eight children, the second youngest being their son, Frederick.

Born on 4 October 1894 at the family home, The Lodge, Bagden Hall, Scissett, Fred attended Scissett Church and sang in the choir; he was also a member of the Denby Dale Band. He worked as a teamer for the Skelmanthorpe Co-Operative Society which entailed driving a team of horses attached to a dray or wagon laden with goods. At the outbreak of the war Fred enlisted with the 7th Battalion Kings Own Yorkshire Light Infantry, he was killed in action on 8 October 1915 aged 21 years. He is buried at Rue du Bois Military Cemetery, Fleurbix.

All-in-One Tree of Frederick Firth

Sergeant Noah Green

Born – Upper Denby 10 December 1891.
Died – France 16 November 1916.
Regimental No. 17744.

Noah Green was the grandson of a Barnsley tallow chandler called
Seth Green, but his roots are very firmly embedded in Denby Dale and
Upper Denby. We begin his family with William Green (1788–1824),
who married Hannah Haworth at Penistone, the couple living at Denby.
Five children were born in the village before William's untimely death
aged only 36. His eldest son, John (1803–1888), was recorded as a fancy
weaver of Denby in 1841, though he was a mason's labourer in 1851.
He married Mary Crossland and had at least six children, all at Denby,
including Seth (1839–1909). It was Seth who moved to Canon Street,
Barnsley, following his marriage to Barbara Smith, circa 1860, who was
originally from Kexborough. In 1861 Seth was noted to be an agricultural
labourer but from 1871 listed his occupation as that of a tallow chandler.

Noah Green, seated bottom right during a break in hostilities for his company.

This was the art of making and selling candles. Historically, candles were made from tallow, a form of animal fat that provided a cheap and efficient way for people to light their homes at night. Seth had at least six children and it is through his son, John Edward (1865–1958), that we continue the line. John married a Denby girl, Lily Barraclough, and nearly all their children were born in the village though the family home was still in Barnsley, on St Johns Road and later on Higham Road in 1911.

John Edward Green 1865–1958.

Noah was born on 10 December 1891 at Denby and was working as a Barnsley corporation gardener in 1911. He joined the war effort by enlisting with the 10th Battalion York and Lancaster Regiment at Barnsley in 1914, aged 22. At some point during his service Noah became a Sergeant, but he died of wounds received in France on 16 November 1916. He is buried at Varennes, Somme, Picardie, France aged 24.

All-in-One Tree of Noah Green

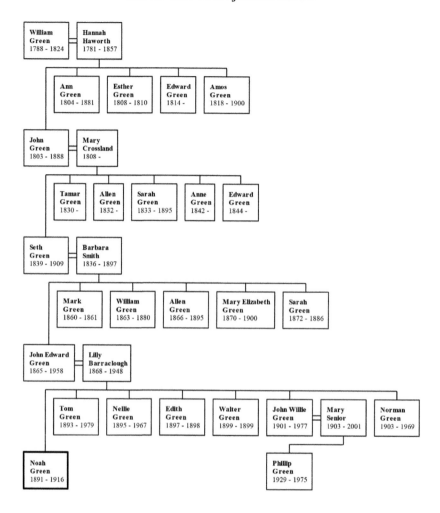

Guardsman Charles Godfrey Hinchliffe

Born – Thurlstone July 1894.
Died – France/Flanders 19 June 1917.
Regimental No. 13956.

Charles Godfrey Hinchliffe has a slightly complicated background but we are able to follow it reasonably well. We will follow his father's ancestry first, which begins with John Hinchliffe marrying Mary Walshaw at Penistone in 1752. Their son, Joshua (1753–1826), died at Carlcoates after having a son of his own, William, at Penistone in 1784. William married Ann Bramall and had John and Charles and it is through Charles (1818–1896) that the descent continues. He married Hannah Day (or Dayes) and had a family of ten children during the period 1842 to 1865. In

1851 Charles was noted to be a stone cutter living at Shepherds Castle, Penistone. This was a pre-historic earthwork (which gave its name to Penistone's Castle Green) and according to historian David Hey:

> marked the boundary between Hunshelf and Oxspring townships where the common of Roughbirchworth met that of Snowden Hill. The earthwork was about 120 yards in diameter, but has been mostly ploughed out except on the Western side.

By 1861, Charles had become a farmer of 28 acres at Thurlstone, in fact the area he farmed was known as Hartcliffe Farm, to the South of Thurlstone and West of Penistone. Charles had expanded slightly by 1871 to 30 acres, and his son, Henry, had become the foreman at a steel works factory. By 1891, Charles was retired and living at Hartcliffe

The grave of William Town and his wife, Anne in Upper Denby churchyard.

cottage but his son, Wright Hinchliffe (1862–1899), who had started out as a farm hand for his father, was head of his own household and farming at Hartcliffe, aged 29. He had married Elizabeth Stanley and she bore him two sons, Wilfred Stanley and Charles Godfrey; all was well set until Wright died at the young age of 37, his sons aged just 9 and 5.

Elizabeth Stanley Hinchliffe coped for the next couple of years, but in 1901 she married Lewis Town, one of thirteen children born to William Town and his wife, Ann Smith. William Town had initially trained alongside his father Jacob (1805–1868), a wheelwright from Ovenden, Halifax. Indeed he is recorded as a journeyman wheelwright in the 1861 census returns, aged 20. But his career was to change considerably when Ingbirchworth Reservoir was completed in 1868. By 1871 (and possibly earlier) William was employed by the local board as the reservoir water keeper, and presumably moved into a reservoir house with his family. In 1881 he was the Ingbirchworth water works manager and in 1891, resident manager of waterworks. He was still in residence in 1911 as waterworks foreman, now aged 70 and close to retirement. We know that he did eventually move out, but only to Upper Denby, where he died in 1924.

Lewis Town (1871–1948) was William's eldest son and a scholar in 1881. By 1891 he was working as a labourer alongside his father at the Reservoir, a position he still occupied in 1901 when he married Elizabeth Hinchliffe. Lewis abandoned the water works before 1911 when he can be found working as a farmer, by now Elizabeth had produced a daughter, Lillian, in 1905 who was to die in 1914 aged only 9. The family was still at Ingbirchworth and Lewis's two stepsons, Wilfred and Charles, are recorded as farm hands in 1911. By 1939, now aged 68, Lewis appears in records from 1939 as a Corn Mill Manager in the Penistone/Thurlstone area.

Charles Godfrey Hinchliffe enlisted for the war as a Guardsman with the Coldstream Guards. Very little is known of his experience of war, other than his end when he was killed in action on 19 June 1917, aged 23. He is buried at Artillery Wood Cemetery and remembered on his father's grave at Stottercliffe Cemetery, Penistone along with the following words:

> Duty called and he was there,
> To do his bit and take his share,
> His heart was good, his spirit brave,
> His noble life he freely gave.

Ingbirchworth Reservoir, circa 1900. Notice the ornate roof on the watch tower.

His brother, Wilfred, also served, this time in the Guards Machine Gun Regiment, his fortune was to return home when hostilities finished. He married Jane Bower in 1918 and can be found living with his brother-in-law, George Bower, aged 70, his wife and a general labourer at Burncote Farm in 1939, when he was described as a farmer – stock rearing. He died in 1982.

All-in-One Tree of Charles Godfrey Hinchliffe

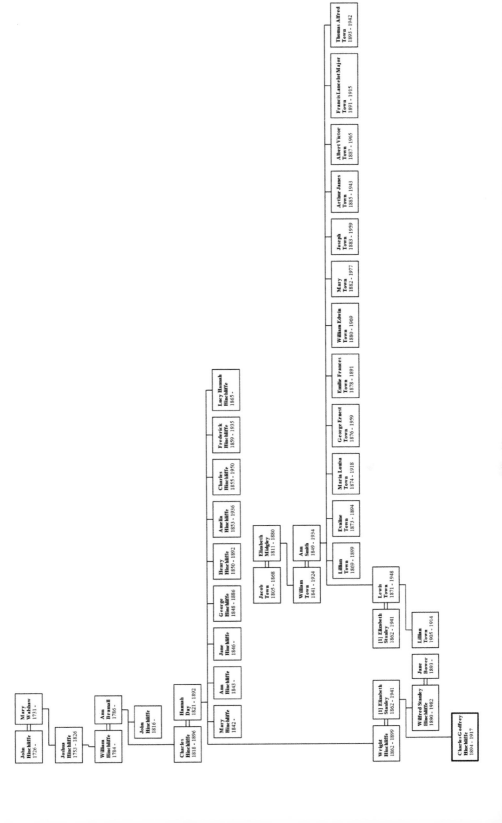

Private Joe Hirst

Born – Upper Denby 19 March 1897.
Died – France/Flanders 29 April 1917.
Regimental No. Po/1146/5.

Joe Hirst was born into a family that had its roots in Cumberworth. William Hirst was born in 1799 and worked as a woollen weaver. He married Mary and had at least five children, all in Cumberworth, including his daughter, Sophia, born in 1847. Here the record goes a little cold. We know that Sophia had a son in 1869 at Cumberworth, but there is no mention of the father's name in the parish baptism records. In the following census returns up until 1881 we find Sophia and her son, John Edward, living with her father William. A marriage was recorded in Cumberworth for a Sophia Hirst to an Absolom Haigh on 14 March 1869, but Absolom then disappears from the record and Sophia Hirst should have been Sophia Haigh – whatever the truth of it we will have to leave it for now.

John Edward Hirst became a platelayer on the railways, rising to the position of Foreman. He married Alice Shipston of Denby and had six children, including Joe, born in 1897, indeed all the children were born at Roebuck Row, Denby. Joe was later recorded in the 1911 census returns as a 14-year-old labourer, prior to enlisting with the Royal Marines Battalion and serving from 26 April 1916 to 14 May 1916 in Ireland during the Easter Rising.

The Rising began on Easter Monday, 24 April, and was planned to be nationwide in its scope, but the British had learned of it which meant it was confined to Dublin. Strategic points in the city were seized by the Irish Nationalists and the Irish Republic was proclaimed. British troops soon arrived to end the rebellion and for almost a week, Dublin was overtaken by street-fighting. Finally, artillery bombardments by the British Army caused the eventual surrender.

Once this was over Joe left English shores again, this time bound for France and Flanders. He embarked on 30 May 1916 and was later drafted into the BEF (British Expeditionary Force) on 3 September, where he remained with the Royal Marine Light Infantry, 190th Brigade, Machine Gun Company until his death on 29 April 1917 when he was killed in action. He is buried at Orchard Dump Cemetery, Arleux-En-Gohelle, to the North East of Arras.

All-in-One Tree of Joe Hirst

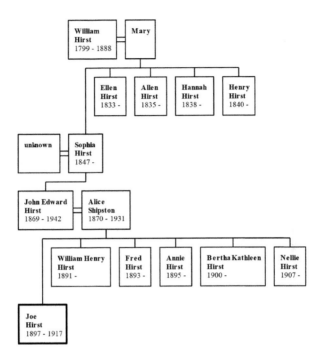

Private Thomas Hodge

Born – Glossop 1890.
Died – The Dardanelles 11 October 1915.
Regimental No. 14190

Details about Thomas Hodge are currently a little thin on the ground. He was born in 1890 in Glossop to Mary Hodge and appears in the 1891 census returns as the only child with his mother. This leads one to conclude that his father had very recently died, or that he was illegitimate and his father was nowhere to be found. His mother was working as a housekeeper in Glossop for Thomas Bennett, a 54-year-old shoemaker originally from Dublin, who was a widower. Mary Hodge lists her place of birth as Falmouth in Cornwall, so she was presumably many miles from her family and friends.

By 1911, Thomas, aged 21, was living as a boarder with retired farmer William Crossland (born 1841–1915) and his wife Mary, at Lower Denby. He worked as a boiler firer at a local plush weaving mill. At the onset of the war he enlisted at Huddersfield as a Private in the 8th Battalion, Duke of Wellington's Regiment. He took part in the Gallipoli campaign and fought in the Dardanelles. This campaign began in February 1915 when the Allies, Britain, France and Russia, tried to weaken the Ottoman Empire by taking control of the Turkish straits and safeguarding the shipping routes through the Suez Canal. In January 1916 the campaign was abandoned and was a very heavy defeat costing 250,000 casualties. Thomas died at the Dardanelles on 11 October 1915.

Private Albert Jackson

Born – Ingbirchworth 10 October 1897.
Died – Flanders 14 July 1918.
Regimental No. R/4/262380.

Albert Jackson was born into a long-established family of farmers. His great-grandfather, John Jackson (1773–1845), worked the land in Cawthorne but his son, George Jackson, was born in Ingbirchworth in 1821. In 1861 he was described as a farmer of 24 acres, but by 1881 he had increased his land to 48 acres in Ingbirchworth. He had also married Mary Ann Haigh from Hepworth and at least six children followed. Their youngest son, also George (1870–1934), followed in his father's footsteps on the family farm, and married Bertha Annie Lockwood at Denby in 1895. The couple had two sons, Fred and Albert, both of whom can be found in the 1911 census returns as 'farmer's son, working on farm'. The family worshipped at the Wesleyan chapel in the village and both sons were baptised there.

Albert enlisted for the First World War and joined the Royal Army Service Corps. This branch of the army was the unit responsible for keeping the British Army supplied with provisions. The exceptions were weaponry and ammunition, which were supplied by the Royal Army Ordnance Corps. At some point during the war Albert became a part of the 2nd Battalion Sherwood Foresters, Nottinghamshire and Derby Regiment, his service number being 73950. He died on 14 July 1918 aged 21 in Flanders and is buried at Nine Elms Cemetery, West Vlaanderen, Belgium. Albert's younger brother, Fred, also joined the war effort. Described as an unmarried farm horseman when he enlisted on 4 June 1918, he joined the Royal Tank Corps (No. 313613) but survived the latter months of the conflict and returned home.

All-in-One Tree of Albert Jackson

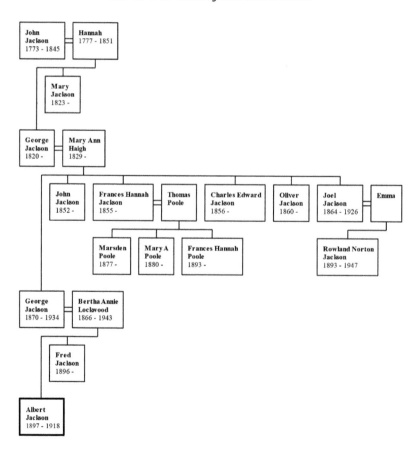

Private Edwin Jackson

Born – Upper Denby 11 October 1897.
Died – France/Flanders 28 April 1917.
Regimental No. PO/1144(S)

Private Herbert Norton Jackson

Born – Upper Denby 17 April 1893.
Died – Bullecourt, France 3 May 1917.
Regimental No. 241594.

The grave of Allen & Martha Jackson in Upper Denby churchyard.

Side panel on the grave of Allen & Martha Jackson commemorating their two sons killed in action in France.

Edwin and Herbert are our second pair of brothers to perish during the war, indeed, they died within five days of one another; one can only imagine the emotions their family felt.

Benjamin Jackson (born 1780) was an Ingbirchworth farmer; he appears in the 1841 census returns though does not appear in 1851. He married Helen Hobson and had a family of at least six children all at Ingbirchworth. It was only natural that his sons would also go into farming; the eldest son, William (born 1806), appears in the 1871 returns as a farmer of 43 acres. The youngest son, Benjamin (1819–1889), also became a farmer in the village; in 1851 he was cultivating 20 acres, though by 1861 this had reduced to 16 acres, and by 1871 it was down to 10 acres. In 1881 the acreage is not given and he is just recorded as a farmer, perhaps the ever decreasing acreage was related to his age, or it could have been financial circumstances. He married Sarah Goldthorpe at Kirkheaton in 1846 and had seven children. We follow the descent through the fourth born, Allen Jackson (1859–1923). The first census taken (1881) after Allen left school finds him working as an indoor farm servant at Ingbirchworth for James Stafford, a farmer of 70 acres, 43 years old, married to Mary (born Denby Dale) with three children. By 1891 he was styling himself as a labourer, both agricultural and for an iron works company. By now Allen was married to Martha Ann Norton and had three children, all at Ingbirchworth. The family also housed a boarder, George Heponstall, a 23-year-old general labourer who was still with them when the next census was taken a decade later. Sometime prior to 1893, Allen and Martha moved the short distance to Richmond Terrace, Upper Denby, where their next six children were born. In 1901 Allen was described as a general farm labourer and also in 1911, although with the detail that he worked for a farmer butcher.

By 1911 the majority of Allen and Martha's children were of working age. Walter was a stonework's operative, Agnes a woollen yarn weaver, Merianne a mohair fringer at a plush works, as was her sister, Mabel. Herbert Norton Jackson (named after his mother's family, who we shall meet again in Appendix 1) was a labourer at a brickworks and his younger brother, Edwin, was a wirer for a mohair weaving company.

Edwin Jackson enlisted for the war with the Royal Marine Light Infantry, 2nd Royal Marine Battalion, Royal Naval Division. He was killed in action on 28 April 1917 and has no known grave. He is commemorated at the Arras Memorial to the Missing.

Herbert Jackson enlisted as a Private in B Company, 2/5th Battalion, Duke of Wellingtons Regiment. He was reported missing at the Battle of Bullecourt on 3 May 1917 aged 24. Like his brother, he has no known grave but is also commemorated at the Arras Memorial to the Missing.

All in one tree of Herbert Norton and Edwin Jackson

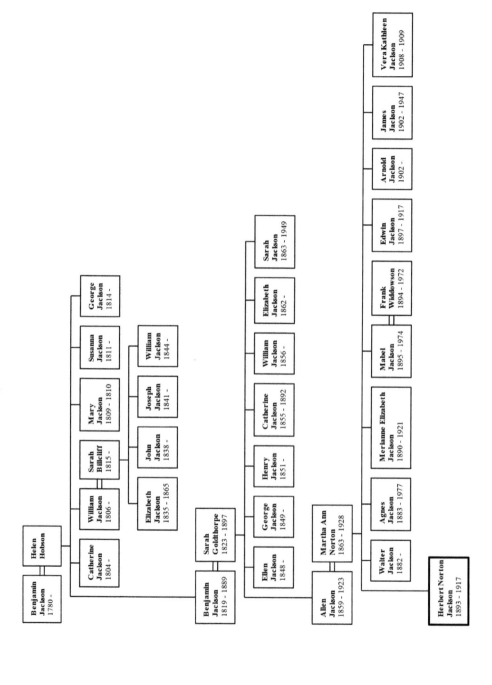

Private Charles Edward Jelfs

Detail of the Jelfs family grave in Upper Denby churchyard commemorating Charles Edward who died in France.

Born – Upper Denby 7 October 1896.
Died – France/Flanders 13 July 1917.
Regimental No. 21470.

Charles Edward Jelfs may have been a Denbier through and through, but his family origins began in Bromsgrove, Worcestershire. James Jelfs (1783–1855) was born in Bromsgrove to Joseph and Mary Jelfs. He married Sarah Hornblower and had ten children; James was always listed in the census returns as an agricultural labourer. His son, Joseph (1825–1891), was noted to be a nail maker in 1861 and 1881, though he had evidently tried something different in 1871 when he was recorded as a butcher and baker. He married Phoebe Emus, and had five children, all in Bromsgrove, and of these two became school masters. Charles Joseph Jelfs qualified as a school teacher in the Bromsgrove district and is recorded in the 1901 census returns with his wife, Mary Alice Chapman, who was an assistant teacher. His younger brother, Abel (1869–1941), also qualified in the Bromsgrove area but unlike his brother, Abel was to travel for his occupation. He married Jessie Heffer (a farmer's daughter) from Stoke by Clare in Suffolk in 1893, before moving north to Upper Denby to take up the position of Head Schoolmaster; Jessie was to be the assistant teacher. It was at the schoolhouse, Denby, that all five of their children were born including Charles Edward in 1896. After retirement, Abel and Jessie moved back to Stourbridge Road, Catshill, Bromsgrove, Abel being buried in Catshill Cemetery after his death in 1941.

Charles Edward enlisted for the war in Hounslow and joined the 1st Battalion, London Regiment. He later served with the Royal Fusiliers W0329 Company in France and Flanders, where he was killed in action on 13 July 1917 aged 20. He is buried at Artillery Wood Cemetery, Boesinghe, Belgium. His younger brother, Clarence Victor, also took part in the war. In 1911 he was boarding with a widow, Susannah Elizabeth Slemaker (Shoemaker) in Walthamstow, aged 16, where he was working as a boy clerk in the Civil Service. He enlisted with the 3rd East Anglian

The Jelfs family grave at Upper Denby churchyard.

Ambulance Regiment in 1915, which then became a part of the Royal Army Medical Corps, his number being 88304. He survived hostilities and returned home to marry Florence Mary Rolph in 1918 at West Ham. In 1939 he can be found working as a staff officer at the Air Ministry in Harrogate and he features in a 1945 edition of the *London Gazette* as a senior staff officer at the ministry of aircraft production. Clarence and Florence retired to the Isle of Wight where Clarence died in 1961.

All-in-One Tree of Charles Edward Jelfs

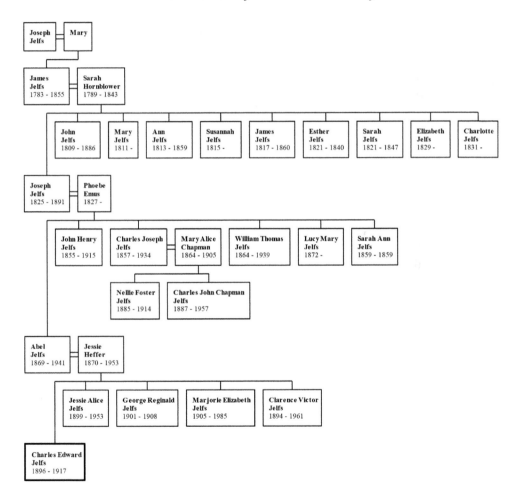

Private James Moore

Born – Upper Denby 8 December 1893.
Died – France 14 May 1915.
Regimental No. 2339.

The family of James Moore can be traced back into the eighteenth century in Upper Denby. James Moore (born around 1769) married Martha Moss in 1786 at Kirkburton, both were noted to be living in Shepley at the time. They had at least eleven children and it would seem that after their wedding they moved to Upper Denby. Their eldest daughter, Maria, was baptised at Penistone (though this could have taken place at Denby and just been recorded in the Penistone register), their second child, Margaret, was baptised at Denby as were the rest of their family. James was a stonemason and at least three of his sons, Miles, Matthew and Michael were apprenticed to their father. It is possible that the eldest son, John, was also a mason, but he died in 1821 aged just 28. Matthew and Miles both worked at Upper Denby, Michael was at Lower Denby. Indeed, a glance through the various parish registers and census returns shows a remarkable number of members of this family working as stonemasons across the centuries.

Miles Moore (1794–1858) married Jane Wood and they had nine children, all at Upper Denby. In 1841 and 1851 the family can be found living on Ratten Row. By 1851, both eldest sons, James and John, had joined the family business. John married Jane Caroline Turton in 1858 at Denby. Jane was the daughter of Thomas Turton, the Denby surgeon and doctor. By 1861 they were living at Ingbirchworth but by 1871 were back in Denby; John remained a mason all his life and all their children were born at Denby according to the census returns. His elder brother, James, married Ellen Crookes, daughter of Ingbirchworth farmer Thomas Crookes at Penistone in 1852. Their family can be found at Upper Denby in all the available census returns. In 1871 Jane (wife of Miles) can be found living with her two unmarried daughters, Jane and Sarah, both working as dressmakers, and next-door-but-one was her son, James, now an employer and described as 'stonemason master, employing four or five men'. The situation was very similar in 1881, by now James's sons were of working age; his youngest, Ernest Thomas, became a monumental mason whose work survives in Denby churchyard and elsewhere. The 1891 census returns record three of James and Jane's sons living at one property in the village, all unmarried and recorded as business partners and stonemasons, these were Matthew Crookes, John Crookes and Ernest Thomas, with Matthew, the eldest, being head of the household. Matthew married Hannah Hardcastle and had two sons before his untimely death in 1898 aged 36. These were, James Moore and his younger brother William. When William married, the entry for his father in the register is deceased, but notes that he had been a builder.

James Moore was born in 1893 and was only 5 when his father died; in 1901 his mother was working as a worsted weaver at a local mill, and in 1911 as a cloth mender to bring in some money to raise her young family alone. There must have been some money around though, as James became a student at St Bede College, Durham, from 1913 until 1915, during which year he enlisted with his friends from college for the war.

The Universities at War website has the following details:

Moore attended Bede College 1913–1915, but is recorded in the *1915 Annual Report* as having already entered military service, and did not complete his studies. He joined 1/8th DLI as Private 2339, and in December 1914 the battalion was based at Sunderland Road Schools in Gateshead. Going to France on 19 April 1915 with the battalion, Moore survived their baptism of fire at Gravenstafel Ridge, during which the unit was reduced to between half and quarter strength, but was killed in action soon after, on 14 May 1915. The battalion had been urgently ordered up into the GHQ Line east of Potijze near Ypres to support some cavalry regiments which had been 'blown out' of their trenches by shell fire, and their trenches lost to German infantry. The GHQ Line at this time stretched from Potijze Wood to a railway station on the Ypres to Roeselare line near Hell Fire Corner. A counter-attack begun at 2 pm retook these trenches, but it was not until another DLI battalion re-dug the degraded trenches on the night of 13–14 May that the position again became tenable, and 8 DLI then moved up into these trenches after 2 am on 14 May. Major Veitch in his battalion history records that the artillery fire that day was lighter than it had been as the battalion had moved up to Potijze, and that Moore was the only man killed that day. The battalion was ordered back to Camp C, Brielen, two days later. Moore is commemorated on the Bede College 1914–1918 *Cross, Plaque*, and *Roll of Honour*, and at *Denby Dale*, Huddersfield.

James Moore was 21 years old and has no known grave. He is commemorated on the Menin Gate Memorial to the Missing in Belgium.

All-in-One Tree of James Moore

Gunner Archie Roberts

Courtesy of Birdsedge Village Hall.

Born – Thurstonland 18 May 1890.
Died – France/Flanders 5 February 1918.
Regimental No. L/28105

Archie Roberts was born to George Roberts and his wife, Mary Jane; George had been born in Braunstone, Rutland where he worked as a farm labourer. By 1885 the family had moved to Stocksbridge and continued to relocate around the area, variously in Honley, Thurstonland, Skelmanthorpe and by 1911, Kitchenroyd. In 1891 George was still recorded as a farm labourer but by the 1901 census was working as an above ground coal hewer, as was his eldest son, Ernest. In all, George and Mary Jane had six children and Archie was born at Thurstonland in 1890. By 1911 he was boarding with George Ernest Kilner and his family on Birdsedge Hill and working in the village as a healder in Furman

Hunt McGrath's textile mill. A healder, or heald knitter, made lengths of cord (healds) with an eye in the middle through which the warp threads on a loom ran so they could be alternately raised and lowered for the shuttle to pass through with the weft thread.

Archie joined up to fight and enlisted with C Battery, 312th Brigade Royal Field Artillery and was killed in action on 5 February 1918. He is buried at Roclincourt Military Cemetery just outside the town of Arras.

All-in-One Tree of Archie Roberts

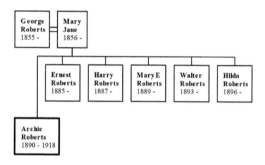

Corporal Joseph Bottomley Rotherforth

Born – Upper Denby 24 August 1894.
Died – Pacaut Wood 15 April 1918.
Regimental No. 14113.

Joseph Bottomley (after his grandmother's maiden name) Rotherforth came from a long established family from Whiston near Rotherham. His great-grandfather, Francis (1806–1886) was a farm labourer here as was his son, John (1836–1905). John had at least eight children, at Whiston but it was the eldest son, George (1857–1901),who broke with tradition and moved away from the village. We can find him in the 1871 census returns, aged 14, working as an agricultural labourer, but it wasn't too long afterwards that he changed course entirely. By the time of the 1881 census returns he had become a Private in the Coldstream Guards and was living in the Old Wing of the Wellington Barracks in Westminster.

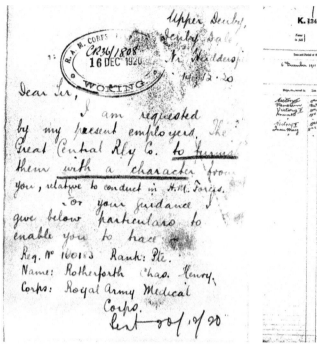

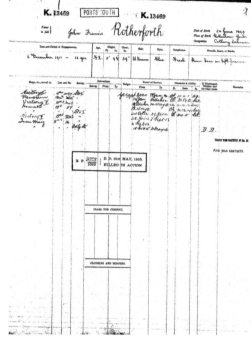

A letter to the army asking for a character reference, written at Denby by Charles Henry Rotherforth in 1920.

The service record of John Francis Rotherforth.

These barracks, built in 1833 are only around 300 yards from Buckingham Palace, which allowed guards to be quickly on hand in case of an emergency. George was discharged from the Guards on 28 February 1882 having completed two years service. Only two months later we find him joining the West Riding Constabulary, on 27 April 1882. There is a brief description of him in the police record, 24½ years old, 5ft 11¼ tall, fresh complexion, light brown hair, mole to the left side of his nose, his warrant number was 4333. By 1886 he was working at Tickhill and by 1890 at Staincross, he had also got married to Mary Elizabeth Bailey in 1886, his first three children being born at Fishlake near Doncaster. The family had moved again by 1891 to Nether Hoyland, south of Barnsley, and then by 1894, to Upper Denby where Joseph Bottomley Rotherforth was born in 1894. George Rotherforth was Denby's village bobby for around seven years before he died in 1901 aged just 44 after suffering a 'cerebral apoplexy', or in today's terms, a powerful stroke.

Joseph Bottomley Rotherforth was a mohair plush weaver in 1911 but he joined the A Company of the 2nd Battalion Duke of Wellington's

Joseph's original wooden cross marking his grave amongst countless others in 1918.

Joseph's grave as it is today.

Regiment and became a Corporal. He was killed in action at Pacaut Wood on 15 April 1918. He is buried at Mont Bernenchon British Cemetery, Gonnehem, France.

Three of Joseph's brothers also served during the war. George William joined the Royal Garrison Artillery as Gunner, No. 151957, his regular employment being a trammer in a clay mine. George did upset the army bigwigs on one occasion when he was given four days in jail for overstaying his leave. Charles Henry joined the Durham Light Infantry, No.160183 and his occupation

George Rotherforth (1857–1901) in his Guards Uniform, circa 1880.

George Rotherforth's grave in Upper Denby churchyard with the memorial inscription recording his son's death in France.

George William Rotherforth (1885–1959, brother of Joseph Bottomley Rotherforth. After the war ended George was noted to be the man in Upper Denby you would go to see to get batteries re-charged for wireless sets and suchlike.

was given as a mill hand. John Frederick (known as Fred) also served in the King's Own Yorkshire Light Infantry. All three brothers survived the war.

A number of cousins also served in the war. These were the children of George Rotherforth's brothers and sisters. Frank Edward Rotherforth had a son, another George (1884–1916), he lived at Wickersley, Rotherham, worked as a gardener and was married with three young children. An Acting Corporal, he was killed in action on 18 January 1916 and is buried at Authuille Military Cemetery, Picardie, France. John Rotherforth had a son, Charles Henry (1889–1948) who lived at Dalton Parva, Rotherham, working as an engine driver. He joined the Yorkshire and Lancashire Regiment (No. 241565) and survived the war. Ann Elizabeth Rotherforth, once of Poplar Terrace, Denby, but back in Rotherham by 1911, had a son, John Francis (1893–1916) who died in the war. Ann Elizabeth later married John William Dawson and John Francis took that as his surname, though the Navy record describes him

All-in-One Tree of Joseph Bottomley Rotherforth

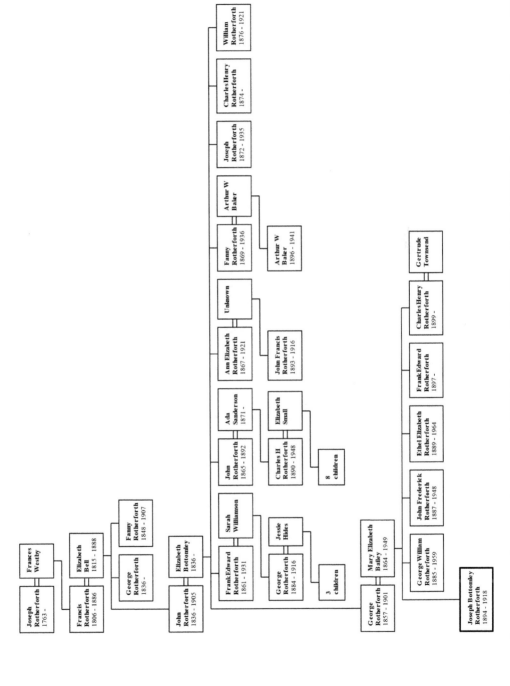

as stepson. John Francis joined the Navy in 1911 and served on the ships: HMS *Victory II*, HMS *Renown*, HMS *Venerable* and HMS *Queen Mary*. He met his death in May 1916 when the *Queen Mary*, engaged in the Battle of Jutland, was sunk with the loss of 1,266 men. Fanny Rotherforth married Arthur W. Baker and had a son, Arthur W. Baker (Junior) 1896–1941. He enlisted for the war in 1914 and became a Corporal in WO 329 Company of the Durham Light Infantry (No. 81597). Charles Henry Rotherforth, finally, George's second youngest brother enlisted in the King's Own Yorkshire Light Infantry as a regular soldier in 1894 aged 21.

Lance Corporal Harry Sheard

Born – Clayton West 4 February 1887.
Died – Italy 15 June 1918.
Regimental No. 23927.

Harry Sheard came from a very old and well established family from Clayton West. Indeed, we can go back to almost the time of the English Civil War with the founder of the family, John Sheard, born in 1657. His son, another John (1695–1764), was born and died at Clayton, he married Maria Revers and had at least five children including one with a most unusual name – Artaxerxes Sheard (1733–1802) was named after the Biblical King of Persia who died in 425BC; he was a younger son of Xerxes I and Amestris and was raised to the throne by the Commander of the Guard, Artabanus, who had murdered Xerxes. We know very little about Artaxerxes Sheard, but we might assume that his father was interested in ancient and Biblical history. Artaxerxes married twice, firstly to Rebecca Broadhead who died a little after the birth of the couple's first child. He then remarried, this time to Mary Berry and had at least a further six children, all at Clayton West. His son, John Sheard (born 1768) married Hannah Firth and had nine children including another Artaxerxes, though he was to be the last member of the family to bear the name. His younger brother, Charles (1795–1873) married Mary Exley and had six children, still all in Clayton West, though most of the records for all the latter are recorded in the High Hoyland Parish registers. Charles worked as a warehouseman from at least 1841, presumably at one of the local textile companies, Beanland's or Norton's perhaps. He had retired by 1871. He was succeeded by his son, John Sheard (1827–1893) who married Elizabeth Lockwood Liles. It would appear likely that John worked with his father as he is also recorded as a warehouseman from 1851 to 1891. John and Elizabeth had four children before her early death in 1873 aged 46. In 1881 John can be found in the census returns employing Mary Eastwood as his housekeeper, but matters altered a few years later in 1886 when he remarried, aged 59, to Emma Walker at Lockwood, Huddersfield. Interestingly, Emma is also recorded as a housekeeper, so whether she took over from Mary Eastwood and a working relationship became something more is a possibility.

John's son, Arthur (1855–1931), married Maria Hinchliffe and had four children. We can follow Arthur through the census returns, he was a scholar in 1861 living at home with his parents, John, a warehouseman and his mother Elizabeth, a fancy wool and worsted loom weaver, the only time her occupation was recorded. Arthur's elder brother, aged 9, was a half-day scholar and half-day worsted bobbin board filler. By 1871, Arthur was working in a local textile factory as a spinner aged 16 and by 1874, he and Maria had begun a family, their home was at Squarefold in Clayton West. By 1891 their two eldest sons, John Thomas and Walter, aged 16 and 14 respectively, were both working as pit labourers. Arthur remained a wool and worsted weaver all his life but by 1901 his youngest son, Harry, aged just 14, was working as an underground coal miner, possibly at the same colliery as his elder brother, John Thomas, who was also a miner.

Harry Sheard (1887–1918) married Olive Smith at High Hoyland church in 1907, the couple having a child, Mildred, in 1910. The 1911

Bilham Grange, Clayton West, circa 1900.

All-in-One Tree of Harry Sheard

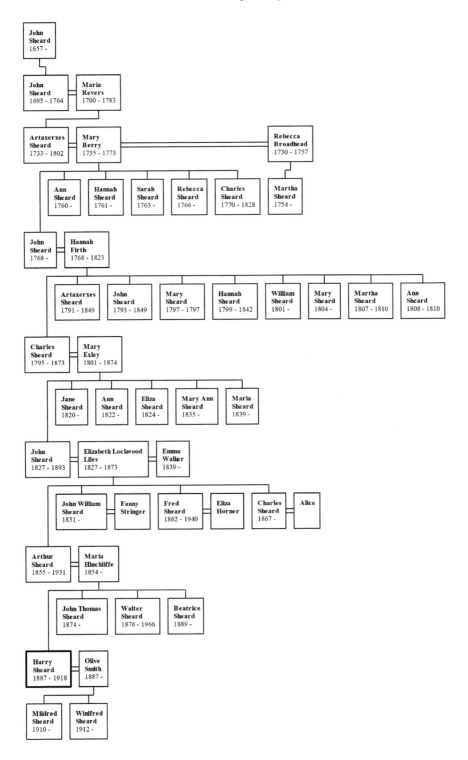

census returns record them living on High Street, Clayton West; Harry, having left the colliery by now, was working as a plush table cover weaver. It is likely that Harry and Olive moved out of Clayton and made their home at Denby sometime prior to the onset of war; Harry is recorded to be working for Denby Dale collieries and also played with the Denby Dale and Clayton West brass bands. They also had another daughter, Winifred, in 1912.

The fact that Harry enlisted for military service at Penistone is further evidence of a move to Denby. This took place in November 1915 and he joined the 9th Battalion York and Lancaster Regiment becoming a Lance Corporal. He was killed in action in Italy on 15 June 1918 aged 34 and is buried at Granezza British Cemetery, Italy.

Private John Walshaw

Born – Netherend, Denby Dale 1 December 1893.
Died – France 27 April 1917.
Regimental No. M2/187879.

John Walshaw came from a farming family background. His great-grandfather, Job (1805–1892) was a farmer in Hoylandswaine and married Mary Roebuck. He can be found in the census returns of 1841 and 1851 as a farmer of 50 acres at West-thorp, and by 1861 his acreage had increased to 60. Job continued farming until at least 1881, by which time he was 76 years old. Naturally his sons followed him into farming, Charles working the land at Birley Carr near Wadsley and the eldest, John (1834–1920), at Netherend Farm, Denby Dale. Prior to this, John can be found in 1861 living at Hill Top, Ecclesfield, and working as an agricultural labourer; he lived with his wife, Hannah Eyre and baby daughter Georgina in their own cottage. Hannah Eyre was born at Hope in Derbyshire and is more than likely to have been of the same family that inspired Charlotte Bronte to write Jane Eyre in 1847. The Eyres were a very old and well established family in the Peak District from at least the thirteenth century and had multiple connections to land and nobility, the famous Yorkshire Civil War diarist, Adam Eyre of Hazlehead Hall, Thurlstone was also likely to be connected.

By 1864 John had moved to his own farm at Netherend and three further children were born here. In 1871 John was noted to be a farmer of 64 acres. As his family grew up the sons took on roles at the farm and by 1911 we find Ernest, now aged 45 and still single, working on the farm alongside his father and his younger brother Joseph (known as Joe) doing the same. Joe was noted to be married to Alice Ollerenshaw and had a young daughter, Georgina, but this was not his first marriage. He had two children before this with Ruthena Lockwood, John (1893–1917) and Charles (born 17 September 1895); two weeks after this event Ruthena had died, it is possible that it was through complications with the birth. As both John and Charles grew up they too became involved with the farm, though John was also employed by Z Hinchliffe & Sons, at Hartcliffe Mills as a motor driver. He was also a scholar at the Primitive Methodist Sunday School on Cuckstool Road, Denby Dale.

John Walshaw enlisted for the war effort in 1916 and embarked for France in June that year. He was killed in action on 27 April 1917, just under a month later his father, Joe, also died. John is buried at Grevillers British Cemetery, France. Many members of this family were buried at Denby and their graves can still be found today.

All-in-One Tree of John Walshaw

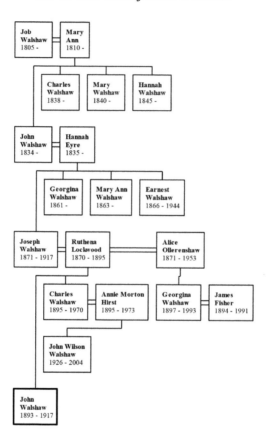

Lance Corporal Arthur Ernest Williamson

Courtesy Birdsedge Village Hall.

Born – Crich, Derbyshire 1890.
Died – France/Flanders 2 March 1916.
Regimental No. 12959

Arthur Ernest Williamson just about scrambles to get onto the Denby fallen list by virtue of his fiancée who lived at Birdsedge. We begin his family with William Williamson who married Jane Wait (1800–1822) and had a son at Yoxall in Staffordshire called John (1821–1876). John, a cotton weaver, married Eliza Jeffrey from Burton on Trent and had eight children including a further William Williamson (1846–1922), who can be found in the 1871 census returns working as a Police Officer, an occupation that lasted until at least 1891, though by 1901 he was described as a farmer. In 1871, aged 25, he had left the family home and was lodging with the Hadfield family in Glossop. By 1881 he was married to Mary Bembridge and living with an ever-expanding family in Barlow near Chesterfield. The family later moved to Crich, also in Derbyshire where Arthur Ernest was born in 1890.

Arthur can be found in the 1911 census returns living with Mary Sadler, aged 53, her daughter, Maria, 31, and three other people all described as servants at New House farm, Birdsedge. Arthur was described as a husbandman and farm labourer. He has also been noted to have lodged with a Mr Fenton Smith of Highfield, Shepley. As stated above, his fiancée lived at Birdsedge, though sadly her name has not yet come to light. He attended, and was also a member of the choir at, Birdsedge Wesleyan Reform Chapel, which may well be where he met her. He had moved to Yorkshire from Fritchley near Crich because he had won a scholarship in agriculture to Leeds University, though by the onset of war he was recorded as living at Heanor, his job being connected with diseases in cattle. He was also noted to have worked for Harris Wood at his brick and tile works in Lower Cumberworth. He enlisted as a Lance Corporal with the 9th Battalion, Duke of Wellington's Regiment, the following newspaper report from the *Derbyshire Times* of 18 March 1916 takes up the story:

> On Friday last week Mr and Mrs Wm. Williamson, farmers at Fritchley, received a letter informing them that their son Lance-Corporal. Signaller Arthur Ernest Williamson of the 9th Duke of Wellington had fallen in action, although this has not yet been confirmed by the War Office. He was 23 years of age, single and was educated at Fritchley School. About twelve years ago he went to work at the farm of the late Mr John Sadler in Yorkshire. Later he worked at a brickyard, also in Yorkshire. He attended evening classes and was successful in winning a scholarship for the Leeds University. Just prior to enlisting he obtained a post connected with cattle diseases at Heanor. He paid a visit to his home in December last on eight days furlough. He enlisted on the 31st August 1914 and had nine months training, after which he went to Flanders, being there eight months altogether. He was killed by a shell in the trenches. He was held in high esteem by his comrades and officers as can be seen by the following and other letters which have been received by his parents:– 'Dear Mrs Williamson, it is with the deepest sorrow and regrets that I write this letter to inform you of the very sad news of your son's death, which occurred on Thursday, March 2nd during a

heavy bombardment by the enemy. We all miss him very much as he was always so cheerful and willing. As for his work, I cannot praise it enough. His courage and fearlessness in the presence of great danger were a fine example to the other men. I may also add that he was on the verge of getting full corporal's stripes and I shall have the greatest difficulty in replacing him. Please accept my deepest sympathy in your very sad bereavement – Yours sincerely, R Dawes, 2nd Lieut. 9th Duke of Wellington's Regiment.

A further report, this time in the *Derbyshire Courier* 18 March 1916 reported:

Crich parish mourns the loss of another of its sons this week, news having been received by Mr and Mrs Wm. Williamson, of Fritchley, that their son, Lance Corporal Arthur E Williamson, had been killed by a shell in the trenches in France. The intimation was conveyed in a letter sent by the sergeant of his company, the signalling section, and bears eloquent testimony to the fine qualities displayed by Lance Corporal Williamson. Dated 4 March, the message reads: 'I think this will be the hardest epistle I have ever sat down to write as it is to inform you kindly how your brave son met his end. It was during the most terrible bombardment that we had ever been in the midst of that it happened. Your boy, Arthur, was taking shelter in a trench when a large shell burst overhead and he was fatally hit. I assure you that he suffered no pain whatsoever as his end was mercifully instantaneous. His loss is most keenly felt by the officers and men of his company and very much felt by our signalling section, as we nearly worshipped him for his fearless and brave actions during any fighting we have taken part in. His last resting place will be marked by a little wooden cross and he is buried side-by-side with several more brave lads who like your son have made the supreme sacrifice for their King and country. I will be pleased to send you any further information which you may desire and which may help to console you in your great loss, which I know you deeply feel. I will conclude with deepest sympathy for myself and everyone of his devoted chums who deeply mourn and regret the loss of one of the best and bravest lads that ever lived, fought and died on the vast battlefield of Flanders. (Signed) Sergeant G England.'

The paper goes on to report:

> Lance Corporal Williamson was born at the old police station, Crich, 25 years ago, his father being the police-officer for Crich. Always possessed with a desire for self-improvement he was of a studious nature, and after passing through the Fritchley School, he moved to Denby Dale Yorkshire and here while employed by the late Mr John Sadler, a prominent agriculturist, he attended the continuation classes and was successful in winning a Leeds University scholarship. Afterwards at Heanor he passed a Civil Service examination under the cattle diseases department. Immediately war broke out he joined the 9th Duke of Wellington West Riding Regiment, and went to France the following July. When over on leave just before Christmas he stated that he had several narrow escapes in the firing line.

Arthur was awarded the Victory, British War and the 1914/1915 Star Medals. After his death his personal effects were distributed as follows:

Soldiers' Effects Book:

Arthur Williamson; 9th West Riding Regt; L/Cpl 12959; killed in action 2.3.16; War Gratuity £6 10s 0d; paid out to:

2.5.16 RP to recharge £1 4s 8d
2.6.16 father William £10 1s 7d
28.8.19 father William £6 10s 0d

Arthur is listed on the Menin Gate Memorial at Ypres.

It is interesting to note that Arthur's brother, George Henry, also followed him into the war. Prior to this he had worked as a domestic gardener. In the army he served as a gunner and he survived to be demobbed and return to Crich.

All-in-One Tree of Arthur Ernest Williamson

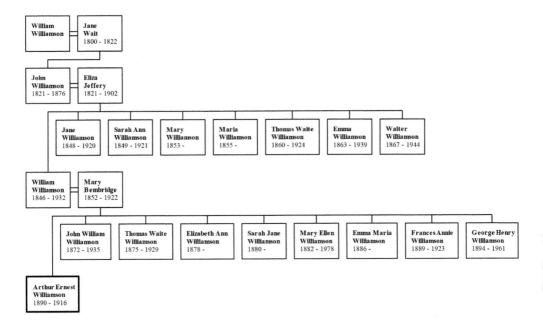

Private John William Wright

Born – Helmsley 1888.
Died – Palestine 21 November 1917.
Regimental No. 82891.

John Wright originally came from a long established family from in and around the North Yorkshire market and castle town of Helmsley. His grandfather, John Wright (1835–1893), was referred to as a gardener's labourer in 1871, long after his marriage to Ursula Sturdy. Their son, William Wright (1857–1898) married Emma Culpan and had four children, all in Helmsley, he was described as an agricultural labourer. Their son, John William Wright, was born in 1888 and left Helmsley sometime before 1911; he was employed initially as a gardener by Mr F.W. Sykes of Green Lane, Lindley, and lodged with a widow, Sarah Ann Crowther, along with her daughter and two other boarders on Wellington Street in Lindley cum Quarmby. It was while living here that John met and married Mabel Atkinson in 1913 and a daughter, Sheila Margaret, was born in 1914. By this time John and his family had arrived in Lower Denby when he was taken on as a gardener by Mr G.W. Wilby of Norcroft, Denby Dale, the family living at Lower Denby.

It is believed that John (height 5ft 2½in tall) enlisted for the war in October 1916 when he joined the 230th Company, Machine Gun Corps which was formerly the Number 37891 York and Lancaster Regiment as a Private. He sailed to Egypt on 1 June 1917 and was killed in action in Palestine on 21 November the same year. He has no known grave but is commemorated on the Jerusalem Memorial to the Missing.

All-in-One Tree of John William Wright

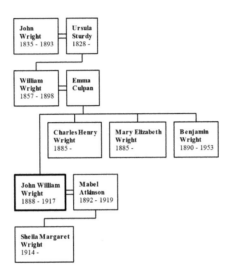

Second World War

Gunner Cyril Schofield

Born – Upper Denby 1919.
Died – Dunkirk 19 May 1940.
Regimental No. 933666

Cyril was a member of a large family that had lived across the Upper Dearne area since at least the late eighteenth century. His great great-great-grandfather, Joseph Schofield (1791–1870) was a farmer of 20 acres on the Skelmanthorpe/Emley border. He and his wife, Sarah Gawthorpe had ten children, all born on the farm, though Joseph's second son Samuel did not follow in his father's footsteps. Samuel was born at Skelmanthorpe (1815–1887) and grew up to become a hand loom fancy weaver, as so many others in the locale were to do. He lived at various times in Kirkburton, Emley, Scissett and Cumberworth where his ten children were born. Samuel and his wife, Harriet Notley Lodge, also had ten children, the eighth of whom was named Lazarus (1852–1910). Biblical names were commonplace in the centuries prior to the twentieth, but Lazarus was unusual even then. Named after Lazarus of Bethany, or Saint Lazarus, who Jesus restored to life four days after his death, our Lazarus had no such lofty aspirations and became a fancy weaver who was living in Upper Denby with his wife, Sarah Ann Hartley, before 1880. Ten appears to have been the magic number of children in these successive generations of Schofields as Lazarus and Sarah also produced ten offspring. Most can be found in the 1911 census returns at Upper Denby. Their eldest child, Louisa, was recorded as being head of the household after the deaths of both her parents under the age of 60. Louisa ran a fish and chip shop business from their home, aided and abetted by younger sister May. Most of the other occupations recorded were based at the weaving mills in Denby Dale, though the youngest son, Ernest, was a boot-maker's apprentice. The seventh-born, Joe Willie Schofield (born 1892), was at this point unmarried and worked as a twister at a local seal and plush manufacturers. In 1917 he wedded Ella Kenyon at Shelley and their son, Cyril, was born at Upper Denby in 1919. In later life Joe Willie retired and moved from Denby to Fylde on the Lancashire coast, where he died in 1972.

Cyril Schofield joined the Second World War soon after its onset when Hitler invaded Poland on 1 September 1939. He became a gunner with the 65th Field Regiment of the Royal Artillery. The war began badly and as the British troops were gradually forced back to the Northern coasts of France, a massive evacuation was organised to take place from the beaches at Dunkirk between 26 May and 4 June. Sadly, Cyril died before this took place on 19 May 1940. From the *Bradford Observer* 1 July 1940:

> Private Cyril Schofield, 21-year-old son of Mr and Mrs J.W. Schofield of Town Gate, Denby was killed in the action on Dunkirk beach states an official notice from the War Office to his parents. He is the first soldier from the Denby area to be killed in action.

He is buried in grave number 35 at Oudenaarde Communal Cemetery in Belgium.

All-in-One Tree of Cyril Schofield

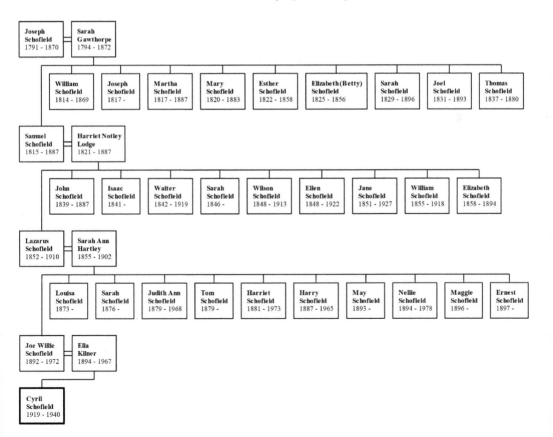

Lieutenant Ernest Roebuck

Born – Ingbirchworth 1920.
Died – Oosterbeek, Netherlands 19 September 1944.
Regimental No. 295263

Ernest's family originated back in the eighteenth century in Thurlstone with Amos Roebuck, who was born in about 1760. He in turn had a son, Enoch (1794–1865), with his wife Mary. In both the 1841 and 1851 census returns Enoch styles himself as a Clothier or Woollen Clothier. By the time of the 1861 census (when he was 67 years old) his occupation is given as a woollen hand loom weaver, perhaps he just couldn't give it up entirely. His family of eight children were all born at Thurlstone, including his seventh born, also called Enoch (1837–1884). This second Enoch was described as a woollen weaver, though by 1881 he had switched his occupation entirely and had become a grocer and draper based at Ingbirchworth. He married Sarah Hanson of Ingbirchworth and had five children the last of which, Edwin, was born at the family home in Ingbirchworth in 1877, which means the move was made after the birth of son Harry in 1873 at Thurlstone, and that the grocer's and draper's business was founded (or taken over) during these four years. Edwin became a joiner and married Mary Turner, the couple going on to have eight children, all born at Ingbirchworth. The family initially resided at the The Cottage, Ingbirchworth, before moving to Ashlea in the village, their youngest son, Ernest, being born in April 1920.

It is not known when Ernest joined the services. We do know that he became a Lieutenant in the 2nd Airborne Battalion in the South Staffordshire Regiment. This regiment was initially an Infantry Brigade but in November 1941 they were converted to a glider infantry role serving in North Africa (1943) and later that year in Sicily, before returning to England in December to prepare for the Second Front. The Battalion went on to play a significant part in Operation Market Garden in the Battle of Arnhem, but here they suffered heavy casualties between 17–25 September 1944. Ernest died here on 19 September and is buried at Arnhem Oosterbeek War Cemetery aged 24.

All-in-One Tree of Ernest Roebuck

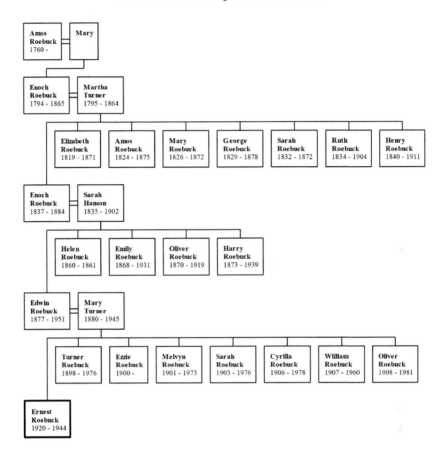

Names of those from the Parish of Upper Denby on Active Service for the King and Country 1939–1945

Arthur Adamson	Robert Emmott	Bessie Heath	Thomas Rusby
Clifford Banham	Jack Fawcett	Evelyn Heath	Herbert Stevenson
Alfred Banham	Bernard Fisher	Norman Laundon PoW	Leslie Shaw
Kenneth Beever	John Gaunt	Cyril Lockwood	Stanley Schofield
Fred Bell	George Gaunt	Jack Lockwood	Harry Swift
George Bower	Francis Grange	John Lockwood	William Shaw
Jim Barber	Arthur Greaves	Roy Lockwood	James Sanderson
Stanley Barber	Roy Harley	Wilfred Lockwood	Cyril Schofield RIP
Douglas Barber	Clifford Horsley	George Moorhouse	Ernest Turton
Laurie Beever	Thomas Haigh	Joe Mosley	Harold Turton
Reggie Beever	Kenneth Haigh	Eric Moxon	James White
Stanley Butcher	Douglas Haigh	Norman Pawson	Arthur Hinchliffe Wilby
Albert Beecroft	Ronald Howland	Rowland Pell	Gordon Wilkinson
Edingell Beever	Ernest Hanwell	Harry Rawdon	Samuel Whitlam
Matthew Dearnley	Edward Hudson	Edward Riggott	Terrence Windle
	Mary Hudson	Donald Rusby	

Private Norman Laundon – Prisoner of War.

No.13022165 Auxiliary Military Pioneer Corps.

Born at Sykehouse, Lower Denby in 1916 to George Redfearn Laundon and his wife, Eliza Jane Watson, one of at least eight children. He was 24 years old in 1940 and was reported missing in action on the official army documents on 19 August 1940. In fact he was captured at Boulogne, fighting in the rearguard in order to help the British troops reach Dunkirk, he was one of the many soldiers who surrendered on 25 May 1940. He was sent, as a prisoner of war (No. 4064) to Stalag 20b, Marienburg, Danzig, Poland. This was originally a camp made from huts and tents with a double boundary fence and watchtowers. As well as British there were also Poles and Serbs being held here. An administration block was built, largely through prisoner labour towards the end of 1940. PoWs were sent out to labour on nearby farms, sawmills, factories, goods-yards and cutting ice on the River Nogat. Eventually Norman's family learned his fate, though it is likely that they were able to write to him. He was kept incarcerated here for five years but was eventually moved out, along with the other 8,000 men held prisoner, due to the forced evacuation undertaken by the Germans in the shadow of the Soviet advance. The following details about one British soldier's experience will give a flavour of the hardships Norman would have had to endure. They come from the diary of one Bombardier Alfred Edward Gray and appeared online in 2004:

20 Jan. 3 a.m. Forced evacuation march from Thorn – 32 kilometres to Schulitz – slept in field of snow.

21 January – 6 a.m. 41k. Bromberg – sleep in garage.

22 January – 32k. Immenham.

23 January – 14k spend night in Fire Station.

24 January – 4k Vanburg.

25 January – 40k big farm outside Flatow

26 January – Receive bread rations and polony.10 p.m. blizzard, march to 6.30 a.m

27 January – 20k sledge breaks down, dump all kit, wet feet. move off 2.30 p.m. 10k.

28 January – Farm. tender skinned and frost-bitten feet.

31 January – 40k gruelling march, hilly roads thick with snow. Boys all in. Still no hot meal.

1 February – 20k to barn. Hope terrible ordeal will soon be over.

The men marched into Northern Poland and then on to Germany with little food, some too weak to carry on. By 16 February they had marched 571km, surviving heavy bombing, and lice for lack of fresh clothing or a wash. By 18 March they had covered 775km in eight weeks, the diary continued to written:

21 March – pass over River Elbe. Pass refugee wagons, 13 dead horses on roadside.

24 March – hundreds of our planes overhead. 26 March – distance marched 926k. CELLE.

28 March – air raids, entrain in goods wagons, 60 men in a wagon, 1 loaf to 6 men, very uncomfortable.

29 March – Spring, split into working groups along railway line.

2 April – Germans pouring back from West. Yanks outside Kassel. German troops rushing from East to stem attack.

7 April – 5 a.m. march 43k through Hanover – people hungry, Jerries deserting.

11 April – Germans flee, only 12 guards.

14 April – Yanks 3k away WE ARE FREE. 16th April – with 2 friends commandeer tractor but halted by blown up bridge. Yank lorry takes us to Hanover. REMEs take us to camp.

17 April – receive bath, delouse, burn all clothing and receive brand new outfit. Good dinner, sent Celle for transport home, three men to room, spring bed!

18 April – 8 a.m. bacon and beans. Over 600 men here waiting for air transport.

22 April – leave in transport planes for Tilburn, change planes, cross Channel in Stirling bomber, Ostend to Clacton, land Aylesbury.

Wonderful reception and tea by WAAFs then to Amersham in lorry to a Reception camp.

The official army report, made on 23 August 1945 was that Norman had been freed, he returned home and lived a full life until his death in 1999.

Fred and George Bower

George Bower, born 1916 to Fred Bower and Eva Martha Boothroyd of 1 Romptickle, Denby Dale, can be found working as a silk power loom overlooker in 1939. His father was a household goods van salesman. The family moved shortly afterwards to Highfield Farm, Denby Dale.

Fred was a veteran of the First World War, born at Wooldale to Eli Bower and Ellen Cartwright, he was noted to be 5ft 3in tall and 33 years and 4 months old on his enlistment form dating from 1917. Eli had been a farmer at Wooldale and later at Netherthong before moving his family to Tenterhouse Farm, Lower Denby.

Fred joined the Duke of Wellington's regiment, No. 205219 and it would seem that by this time he had abandoned Tenter House farm, though his father can still be found here in 1911. He lists his occupation as that of a hawker on the enlistment paper. He was also married by now, to Eva Martha Boothroyd, the ceremony taking place at the Independent Chapel, Thurlstone in 1915, the couple lived at 1 Romptickle, Denby Dale. Fred was recorded to be at home between 11 April to 2 August 1917, but on 3 August he left to join the British Expeditionary Force in France. He was also a new father as his son, George, had been born on Boxing Day 1916.

George was noted to be a power loom overlooker in 1939, still living at home, Fred was by now recorded as a household goods van salesman. George enlisted for the Second World War at its onset. He joined the

All-in-One Tree of George Bower

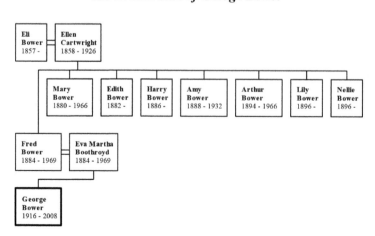

Royal Navy and served on the aircraft carrier HMS *Eagle*, taking planes to Malta.

HMS *Eagle* was built by Armstrong Whitworth at Clydebank and laid down in February 1913. It was launched on 8 June 1918 and was sunk on 11 August 1942 by four torpedoes from the German submarine *U73* while escorting a convoy to Malta. Two officers and 158 ratings lost their lives but 927 of the ship's crew were picked up by HMS *Laforey*, HMS *Lookout* and the tug, *Jaunty*. The wreck is in the Mediterranean, seventy nautical miles south of Cape Salinas, Majorca.

George and the rest of the survivors spent two hours in the sea before the rescue was effected and they were taken to Gibraltar.

The Lockwood Brothers

Three brothers from Pinfold at Denby fought in Second World War – Jack, Roy and Cyril Lockwood; they were members of a family with roots well back into the eighteenth century in the Denby area. The earliest forebear of the line currently known is Thomas Lockwood, born in 1658 at Almondbury, he was followed by his son, John, born 1685 at Kirkheaton, and he by his son, Thomas, born in 1710 at Mirfield. Thomas's son, Joshua (born 1738), was the first member of the family to be associated with Penistone in the records and by Penistone we might understand it to actually be Denby as all records were recorded in the Penistone registers at this time. We can find Joshua paying land tax in the late eighteenth century through to at least 1813 to owners including Sir George Savile, Thomas Kaye and (widow) Ann Wrigley all for parcels of land at Denby.

Joshua's son John, born in 1759, provides us with more details. The family were one of a number farming lands at Denby Hall, once the home of the former Lords of the Manor, the Burdett family, who had sold up to the Savile family in 1643. John married Diana Haigh at Penistone in 1789 and spent the rest of his life farming these lands, eventually passing them on to his son, Benjamin, after his death in 1834, he is buried at Penistone.

Benjamin Lockwood (1794–1846) married Hannah Marsden at Penistone in 1828 and had at least eleven children. He can be found in 1841 farming at Denby Hall living in the family home with his now widowed mother, Diana, aged 70, who died the following year. Benjamin was not destined for old age and died shortly after, aged 52, but his wife retained the family business and is recorded in 1851 as a farmer of 58 acres at Denby Hall, now assisted by her sons Thomas and John. Hannah was still here in 1861, now assisted by more of her maturing offspring, John, Henry, Benjamin and Edward, the farm now being 68 acres in size. Hannah's younger brother, David Marsden, was also living here and employed as a farm labourer. The farm size increased again prior to 1871 when it was recorded as 78 acres, Hannah was still head of the family, though was now living with just her sons: Henry aged 31, and Edward aged 24, both farm labourers. Her son John had left to begin his own farming operations by now and can be found with his family at Wheatley

Hill, Clayton West, where he was recorded as a farmer and thresher. The family can still be found here in 1881, though by now, Hannah was 75 years old and had been a widow for 35 of them. Henry was still working on the farm as was her youngest son, Edward, he was the steam engine driver and was by now married himself. Meanwhile, John Lockwood had left Wheatley Hill and moved back to Nether Denby, only a stone's throw from his parental home, with his family, still working as a farmer. Hannah died in 1882 and it would seem that John may have taken on a role at the family farm himself because in 1891 he was back at Denby Hall, in the census returns of that year he was recorded as a threshing machine proprietor. His brother Henry and elder sister Sarah were also living here and are recorded as being next door. Edward had by now moved on to his own farm at Upper Bagden, again, just a short distance from his family home. He had married Elizabeth Heeley of Cawthorne in 1874, the couple having at least seven children, all of whom can be found living and farming at Upper Bagden in the next two census surveys of 1901 and 1911. Edward died in 1912 and it is through his son, John, that we follow the line.

Edward Lockwood (1846–1912).

Seated on the right, Maude Wood (1892–1952) who married John Lockwood.

Pinfold, the Lockwood family home from at least 1938.

John Lockwood (1886–1953) in his steam roller overalls with Maude and two grandchildren.

John married Maude Wood in 1912 at Denby church where he is still described as a farmer. The family were living at Sykehouse, Lower Denby by 1923 though they moved again, sometime prior to 1938, after which date they lived at Pinfold, Upper Denby. John also abandoned the farming life and for many years worked as a steam roller driver for the local authority. The couple had six children and it is with the three brothers mentioned above that we are concerned here.

Jack Lockwood (1919–1966)

Jack Lockwood in full Highland Light Infantry military uniform outside the family home, Pinfold.

A more formal studio photograph of Jack Lockwood in Highland uniform.

Jack (No. 3317848) joined the Highland Light Infantry and served with them from 20 October 1939 to 30 November 1940. From then he was with the Royal Armoured Corps serving in the North African campaign, and then Italy from 1 December 1941 to 3 June 1946. It is interesting to note that Jack's letter home to his mother Maude made the local newspaper:

Together in Italy.
Mr and Mrs J Lockwood, of Pinfold, Upper Denby, have had news that their eldest and youngest sons have met in Italy. Trooper Jack Lockwood, the elder, has been in the Army four years. He has been on active service since August 1942 in Egypt, through North Africa and into Italy, where he met his brother, Cyril, who is serving in the Royal Engineers.

Jack Lockwood, sat on the right of the tank.

Cyril has had two years service and went to North Africa nearly twelve months ago. In his letter, Jack told his mother that Cyril both looked and felt well. They had met quite unexpectedly, but only for half an hour. It was the first time Jack had seen Cyril in khaki. Another brother, Roy, has been serving in the Navy for four years. He once spent five hours in the sea when the ship on which he was serving was sunk while on convoy duty to Russia.

Jack in more practical military wear during the war.

Roy Lockwood (1921–1997)

Roy joined the Royal Navy and in April and May 1942 was on board the HMS *Punjabi*.

HMS *Punjabi* was deployed on 26 April to provide distant cover for the passage of Convoy PQ 15. They sailed from Hvalfjörður on 29 April, on 1 May she was rammed and sunk in a collision with the battleship HMS *King George V* in foggy conditions. While sailing in formation in heavy fog, the lookout on the *Punjabi* reported what he

HMS *Punjabi* before the accident.

Bows That Cut Destroyer In Two

AFTER her collision with the destroyer Punjabi, which was cut in half, Britain's monster battleship, King George V, lay-to in an Icelandic fiord for emergency repairs before being taken to the Gladstone Dock, Liverpool. Bottom picture gives a close-up of the huge hole torn in her bows, while the larger picture gives a general view of the damaged battleship.

Rode 1,750 Winners

CHARLES WOOD who died

A contemporary newspaper report about the collision.

believed to be a mine dead ahead; the captain ordered a fifteen point emergency turn to port; in so doing, she sailed directly into the path of *King George V* and was sliced in two by the battleship's bow. 169 of the ship's company were rescued from the forward section, and another forty were picked up from the sea by other escorts, including *Marne*. The crew left in the aft section, which sank very quickly, were killed when her depth charges detonated; forty-nine men lost their lives in the accident. She sank directly in the path of the US battleship USS *Washington*, which had

Preparing for the 1947 Royal Tournament, Roy Lockwood is third from the left.

to sail between the halves of the sinking destroyer. *Washington* suffered slight damage from the detonation of the depth charges. *King George V* sustained serious damage to her bow, and was forced to return to port for repairs. Further investigation revealed no mines in the area, or indeed in any part of the convoy's eventual path. It was unknown what the lookout actually spotted, if anything.

Roy spent five hours in the water awaiting his eventual rescue. After the war, Roy took an active role in the Royal Tournament at Olympia in London 1947. He later emigrated to Australia.

Cyril Lockwood (1923–2001)

Cyril joined the Royal Engineers for the war effort and as we have seen above met up with his brother in Italy. Cyril (No. 2154459) served from 22 January 1942 to 24 February 1947 when he was transferred to the Army Reserve. On his return home Cyril joined the Denby Dale branch of the British Legion.

Cyril Lockwood in uniform during World War Two.

Cyril Lockwood's membership booklet of the Denby Dale branch of the British Legion.

Denby school children in the playground, around 1930. Back row, 2nd from left is Cyril Lockwood and back row 2nd from right is Roy Lockwood.

May Lockwood, eldest sister of the Lockwood brothers.

Maude Lockwood with a grandchild in the doorway at Pinfold. Just above the letter box is a sign that says Air Raid Warden, as all three sons were involved in the war this must refer to John Lockwood.

Jack Lockwood's wedding to Mary Derwent in 1949 at Midhope. Back row, left to right: Cyril Lockwood, John Lockwood, Jack Lockwood, Margaret Mary Derwent, Sybil Cherry, Clarence Cherry, ?, Cyril Cherry. Front row, left to right: Tony Cherry, Maude Lockwood, Hilda Cherry.

Cyril Lockwood's wedding to Gwendoline Wood in 1945 at Helme Church. Back row, left to right: John Lockwood, Jim Cuncliffe, Cyril Lockwood, Gwendoline Wood, James Wood, Hildred Haigh. Front row, left to right: Miss Smith, Maude Lockwood, Roy Turner, Alice Wood, Henry Turner, Megan Sykes.

All-in-One Tree of Jack Lockwood

The Fallen of Denby Dale and Cumberworth Parish

First World War

Ralph Armfield (1895–1917)

Courtesy Birdsedge Village Hall.

Private. No. 34258. Leicestershire Regiment. Transferred to Number 41593 Lincolnshire Regiment. Awarded Victory and British war medal. Ralph was the son of George Armfield and Minnie Taylor and in 1911, aged 16, was recorded in the Ardsley district of Barnsley working with his father as a milk seller. He was wounded on 1 September 1917 during the war, but on 29 September 1917 he was reported as wounded and missing. Possibly as a result of the confusion of war a death date of 31 July 1917 was recorded, it is possible this was meant to read 30 September. His next of kin was noted to be living at an address in Denby. In 1927 a Frank and Ruth Armfield were recorded in Upper Denby church registers as having had a daughter, Phyllis. The family lived at Green Lane End Farm, High Flatts and interestingly, Frank was a milk dealer. It was a marriage between cousins, Frank was the son of Charles Armfield (1864–1950), and Ruth was Ralph's sister, daughter of George Armfield (1861–1938), the two youngest sons of Joseph Armfield and Charlotte Grover. Ralph was perhaps working on the farm and living here which explains his name being on the Denby Dale War Memorial.

Mark Atkin (1898–1916)

Private. No. 6666 later 512757. 1/14th (County of London) Battalion, London Scottish. He was the son of Amos and Jane Elizabeth Atkin of West Cliffe Lodge, Denby Dale. Amos was born at Horncastle, Lincolnshire, and worked as a groom and gardener, his wife originated in Ripon. In 1911 the family lived on Dearne Terrace, Denby Dale; Mark was 13 at this time and was employed as a worsted spinner, his siblings were Susan Beatrice (worsted spinner), Ethel, and Kathleen (who was born in Denby Dale). The family once lived at West Cliffe Lodge, where Amos was head gardener. Mark was killed in action on the first day of the Battle of the Somme, 1 July 1916, aged 18, and is commemorated on the Thiepval Memorial to the Missing.

Clifford Thomas Sydney Cunningham (1897–1916)

Private. No. 240267. 1/5th Battalion Duke of Wellington's Regiment. He was born at Hoyland Common. Lived at Denby Dale, the son of Police Constable William Cunningham and Elizabeth Cunningham. William, originally from Lincolnshire, had served as a police officer in Tankersley and Staincross prior to his move to High Street, Denby Dale. His children were all involved in the textile industry, John was a cloth finisher, Bernard a cloth warehouseman, Llewllyn a wool piecer and Clifford was employed at G.H. Norton's, Scissett. He embarked for France in April 1915 and was reported missing 3 September 1916. He has no known grave but is commemorated on the Thiepval Memorial to the Missing.

Harry Ellis (1898–1917)

Courtesy Birdsedge Village Hall..

Rifleman. No. 51911. 2/8th Battalion West Yorkshire Regiment. Born at Cumberworth, he was the son of Allen and Lucy Ellis of Crosspipes, Birdsedge. Allen (1863–1937) was originally from Ardwick, Lancashire, but arrived in Birdsedge after his marriage to Lucy Broadbent who was born at Denby; the marriage took place at Cumberworth in 1888 where both participants were recorded as weavers. Although the address regularly given was Crosspipes the family home was actually at Park Head Row. Allen worked as a plush weaver in 1891, a stone quarry delver in 1901 and a fancy worsted weaver in 1911. Their family began with the birth of Percy (1889–1949) and continued with Evelyn (1891–1977), Tom (1893–1977), Marion (1897–1960), Harry (1898–1917), Fred (1901–1967), Edith (1903–1981) and Nelly (1905–1983). All can be found in the 1911 census returns where Percy, Evelyn and Marion were all employed as fancy worsted weavers. Tom was a woollen feeder. Harry was still a scholar at this date. Harry enlisted for the war as number 51911 with the Prince of Wales' Own West Yorkshire Regiment 2/8th Battalion, Leeds Rifles 62nd Division. A report dated 30 March 1917 states he was transferred to a sick convoy with diarrhoea. He was reported missing on 11 January 1918 and confirmed killed or died of wounds by the German Government on 23 July 1918. He actually died at the Battle of Cambrai on 22 November 1917 aged 19. He has no known grave but is commemorated on the Cambrai Memorial to the Missing.

Tom Ellis (1894–1977)

Courtesy Birdsedge Village Hall..

Able Seaman. No. J68661. Royal Navy. Tom was the brother of Harry Ellis noted above. On his enlistment form dated 15 March 1917 he was noted to be 5ft 5½in tall, with brown hair, blue eyes and a fresh complexion. He joined the Royal Navy and the first ship he sailed on was the *Pembroke*. His service ended on 25 February 1919 and the final ship he served on was the *Mantua*. He returned home and founded a green grocer's business in Birdsedge. In 1925 he married Ethel Hutchinson (1895–1962) at High Hoyland and had two children, Pauline M. Ellis (born 1929) and Jean M Ellis (born 1931). In 1939 the family were at Thread Mill Farm, Birdsedge where Tom was now described as a farmer.

Sam Ellis (1886–1916)

Private. No. 25398. 6th Battalion York and Lancaster Regiment. He lodged with Mr Joe Field, Commercial Road, Skelmanthorpe. He worked as a mason at Cook and Heywood, contractors, Cumberworth. In 1911 he can be found living at High Flatts with his sister, Ada when he notes his occupation to be a bricklayer, both siblings were born in Manchester and were single. Sam enlisted in April 1916 and was killed in action on 22 August 1916, he is buried at the London Rifle Brigade Cemetery, Ploegsteert.

Arthur England (1881–1917)

Private. No. 4741. 2/5th Battalion York and Lancaster Regiment. He was born at Penistone and lived at Cumberworth. He was the son of Ben and Janet England. Ben England was recorded as a grocer and draper at Cumberworth in 1891 and the business was carried on after his death by his wife in the record from 1901. The couple had at least seven children, Arthur, Jonathan, Charlotte Elizabeth, Eva, Joseph, Marian and Alice. In the 1901 survey Jonathan and Joseph were both apprentices to a tailor. Arthur was working in the family business as a carrier between Huddersfield and Cumberworth. He was also a member of the Cumberworth Wesleyan Reform Choir. Arthur enlisted in March 1917 and died of wounds at No. 4 Casualty Clearing Station 7 March 1917 aged 36. He is buried at Varennes Military Cemetery.

Jonathan England (1884–1917)

Private. No. 38232. 15th Battalion (1st Leeds Pals) West Yorkshire Regiment. Born at Fulstone he was the son of Elliott and Ellen England. Elliott was born at Fulstone and was a stonemason/quarryman, Ellen was born at Cumberworth. All their children were born at Fulstone but Jonathan ended up living in Upper Cumberworth and married Bertha Riding (of Church View, in the village) in 1907. The couple had a child, Aden Elliott England who was three weeks old when the census was taken in 1911, Jonathan was a stonemason. He was killed in action at Gavrelle during the Battle of Arras 3 May 1917. He has no known grave but is commemorated on the Arras Memorial to the Missing.

Arthur Firth (1892–1917)

Private. No. 19932. 6th Battalion King's Own Scottish Borderers. Born at Cumberworth, the son of George Thomas Firth and Emma Horn of Upper Cumberworth. He was educated at Leeds College and was a teacher at Garforth Council School. Enlisted May 1915. Arthur was killed in action 3 May 1917 aged 24. He has no known grave but is commemorated on the Arras Memorial to the Missing.

Horace Firth (1886–1918)

(Served under the name of Depledge.) Sergeant. No. 842282. 24th Battalion Canadian Light Infantry. Born in Denby Dale to Amos and Louisa Firth, he emigrated to the United States in 1907, arriving in New York from Liverpool. At the outbreak of the war he travelled from California to British Colombia, Canada to enlist. He joined the Canadian navy and served for a while as an able seaman on board the *Niobe*. He was dissatisfied by encountering no action and transferred to the infantry. He was awarded the Military Medal in December 1917. He died of wounds on 25 February 1918 aged 30 and is buried at Barlin Communal Cemetery Extension.

George Edward Gibson (1896–1918)

Courtesy Birdsedge Village Hall..

Private. No. 64010. 11th Battalion The Welsh Regiment. George was born at Birdsedge to George Edward Gibson (1870–1955) and Fanny Thompson (1875–1925). George Edward senior (a groom/coachman) was originally from Lincolnshire but married Fanny at Pudsey in 1895, she was a native of Dent in the Yorkshire Dales. George Edward junior was born at Pudsey but after 1903 his siblings were all born at Birdsedge. These were: Annie (1897–1955), Harry (1899–1953), Bertha (1901–1996), Walter (1903–1962), Arthur (1905–1984), Willie (1907–1977) and Mary Elizabeth, known as Lizzie (1909–1939). In 1911 George was working in a woollen mill while his father was noted to be a coachman. George enlisted with the Royal Army Medical Corps (No. 76249) before he became a soldier with the Welsh Regiment (No. 64010). He was killed in action in Salonika, Greece 18 September 1918 aged 22 and buried at Doiran Military Cemetery, Greece.

Willie Heeley (1892–1918)

Private. No. 38654. 1/5th Battalion York and Lancaster Regiment. Willie was born at Denby Dale; the son of Thomas Heeley (born 1860) and Mary North (born 1869). Tom and Mary both worked in the local weaving industry. The 1911 census returns note their children to be Edwin (a weaver), Willie (a cloth finisher) and Harry (a scholar) the family living on Norman Road, Denby Dale. Willie married Francis Lockwood (1892–1948) at Cumberworth in 1912 where his occupation is given as a cloth finisher, his father was recorded as a teaser in a local mill. Willie enlisted at Penistone in the Yorkshire and Lancashire Regiment but later became part of the 20th Tyneside Scottish Regiment (No. 48332) and was killed in action 15 April 1918 and buried at Cabaret Rouge British Cemetery.

Ben Howard (1896–1918)

Private. No. 270584. 2nd Battalion, The Royal Scots. Formerly No. 270584 York and Lancaster Regiment; No. 240986 Scottish Rifles. Ben was born and lived in Denby Dale, the son of Walter and Sarah Howard. By 1901 Walter had died leaving his wife to become a charwoman. By 1911 while living at Dearne Terrace, Sarah is recorded with her children: John (aged 25 a fettler of scribbling engines), George Walter (aged 22 a spinning weaver), Granville (aged 20 an assistant teacher), Percy (aged 17 a bobbin carrier) and Ben (aged 15 a joiner and wheelwright's apprentice). Ben died of wounds on 22 March 1918 aged 22 and was buried at Bac-du-Sud British Cemetery.

George Neaverson Hoyland (1893–1917)

Trooper. No. 2392. Royal Horse Guards. He was born at Cumberworth, the son of Elizabeth Sharpe Hoyland (nee Neaverson) of High Street, Denby Dale and the late Albert Edward Hoyland. Albert Edward was a certificated schoolmaster and taught at Cumberworth school, assisted by his wife. Their children recorded in 1911 were as follows: Gertrude Mary (an assistant teacher at Cumberworth), Charles Ernest (an office boy at a solicitors) and George who worked as a railway clerk. George was involved in the war by June 1916 and was wounded in his left arm on 6 November 1917. He died of wounds on 8 November 1917 at No. 10 Casualty Clearing Station aged 24 and was buried at Lijssenthoek Military Cemetery.

Harry Kaye (1882–1917)

Corporal. No. 240266. 2/5th Battalion Duke of Wellington's Regiment. He was the son of Joseph and Ann Kaye of Lane Head, Hinchliffe Mills near Crow Edge a few miles to the West of Birdsedge. Harry was a traction engine driver in a stone quarry, possibly working alongside his father who was a quarryman. He was killed in action at the Battle of Bullecourt 3 May 1917. He has no known grave but is commemorated on the Arras Memorial to the Missing.

Tom Crowther Littlewood (1893–1917)

Private. No. 28457. 18th Battalion West Yorkshire Regiment. He was born at Skelmanthorpe, the son of Clara Littlewood who was described as a spinster, though Clara had in fact been married (in 1895) to Joseph Beaumont and can be found living with him at Ossett in 1901. By 1911 Joseph had died and Clara and Tom can be found living with the family of

Walter Morley (a labourer and carter), at Garrett Buildings, Cumberworth Road, Skelmanthorpe. Walter Morley had married Jane Senior who had children from a previous marriage to Granville Lockwood (died 1878) as she was noted to be 'widow Littlewood' and so Clara was Walter's step daughter. Tom Crowther Littlewood was living at Garrett Buildings with his grandfather in both the 1901 and 1911 censuses and was noted to be a plush weaver. He married Narah Peace of Cumberworth on Boxing Day 1914 by which time Tom was working as a miner. It would appear that they moved to Birdsedge and had a son, Walter in 1915 prior to Tom enlisting for the war. Tom embarked for France September 1916, but was gassed the following month and died of wounds 30 April 1917 aged 22. He is buried at Aubigny Communal Cemetery.

Tom Crowther Littlewood's grave at Aubigny today.

Jane Senior, Grandmother of Tom Crowther Lockwood.

Thompson Lockwood (1888–1916)

Private. No. 14192. 9th Battalion Duke of Wellington's Regiment. Born in Denby Dale, the son of Henrietta and the late Charles Lockwood (a teamer of horses), of High Street, Denby Dale, and also Revel Bottom in 1891. He was employed as a collier at Naylor's colliery, Lower Denby. He was also a keen athlete and a member of Denby Dale cricket club. He was reported missing in a bayonet charge on 2 March 1916 aged 28. He has no known grave but is commemorated on the Menin Gate Memorial to the Missing.

James Willie Peace (1882–1918)

Private. No. 32424. 2nd Battalion York and Lancaster Regiment. He was born at Gledholt Bank, Huddersfield, the son of James Walter and Elizabeth Peace. He married Norah Novello Dearnley at Upper Cumberworth in 1910, the couple lived on Church Street in the village and had two daughters, Lillian born in 1910, and Dorothy born in 1913. Norah was originally from Ingbirchworth where her father, Wright Dearnley, worked as a mason. James worked as a plush weaver prior to enlisting for the war at Penistone on 11 December 1915, when he entered the training reserves. He was killed in action 21 March 1918. He has no known grave but is commemorated on the Arras Memorial to the Missing.

Stanley Peace (1892–1917)

Private. No. 14193. 10th Battalion Duke of Wellington's Regiment. He born at Cumberworth, the son of Herbert and Mary Peace, Old Post Row, Cumberworth. The family can later be found at 1 Sunside Cottages, Birdsedge. Stanley was employed at Naylor Brothers pipe-works in Denby Dale. After enlistment he was reported missing on 5 November 1916 and wounded on 13 November 1916. He was killed in action at Passchendaele on 20 September 1917 aged 25. He has no known grave but is commemorated on the Tyne Cot Memorial to the Missing.

John Pitchfork (1899–1918)

Private. No. 34978. 9th Battalion Duke of Wellington's Regiment. Formerly No. 38958 East Yorkshire Regiment. He was born at Hooton Pagnell, near Doncaster; the son of Martha Ann Pitchfork (née Waddington) of 3 Pickford Square, Milnsbridge. His father Charles (a farmer) had died before 1911, by which time the family had moved to Croft Terrace, Denby Dale. John was killed in action 4 November 1918 aged 19 and buried at Poix-de-Nord Communal Cemetery.

Cornelius Thomas William Rigby (1874–1916)

Private. No. 3/11375. 10th Battalion Duke of Wellington's Regiment. He was the son of Rev. Thomas Newton Rigby and his wife, Sarah Elizabeth Lees. The family can be found living at Trinity Road, Handsworth, in 1881; Thomas was a Clergyman without his own parish and father to four children, Cornelius, Florence, Annie and Harriet. Sarah Elizabeth died in early 1884 and by 1891 Thomas had moved his family to Skipton. By 1901 Thomas had moved again, this time to Field House, Denby Dale, along with Cornelius and Annie, who was described as the family's housekeeper. Cornelius was a dealer in cattle medicines and in 1911 he was more broadly described as a veterinary medicine dealer. He enlisted for the war in Huddersfield and can be found in France on 6 October 1915. He was killed in action at Munster Alley near Poitieres during the Battle of the Somme on 29 July 1916 aged 42. He has no known grave but is commemorated on the Thiepval Memorial to the Missing.

Willie Schofield (1893–1918)

Private. No. 202897. 4th Battalion South Staffordshire Regiment. He was born in Denby Dale, the son of Albert and Lucy Ellen Schofield and lived on Sunny Bank, he worked as a cotton finisher in one of the local mills. Willie was killed in action near Rheims on 31 May 1918 aged 24. He has no known grave but is commemorated on the Soissons Memorial to the Missing.

Ernest Thackra (1894–1918)

Private. No. 204478. A Company, 9th Battalion Duke of Wellington's Regiment. He was the son of George and Ann Thackra of Wesley Terrace, Denby Dale. Employed at G.H. Norton's, Nortonthorpe Mills, Scissett. He was a member of the local territorials prior to the outbreak of the war. In 1901, the family were living at Dunkirk, Denby Dale, and the 1911 census records Ernest as an overlooker at a cotton spinning mill. He embarked for France in 1916 and was wounded three times. He died of wounds received during the attack on the Canal du Nord on 21 October 1918 aged 24. He is buried at Rocquigny-Equancourt Road British Cemetery.

Clarence Edward Widdowson (1892–1916)

Private. No. 14490. 10th Battalion Duke of Wellington's Regiment. He was born at Cumberworth, the son of Henry and Alice Jane Widdowson who later moved to Hillside, Denby Dale. He was employed at Stringer and Jaggers colliery at Emley Moor as a clay trammer. Clarence was killed in action at Munster Valley on 29 July 1916 during the Battle of the Somme, aged 24. He has no known grave but is commemorated on the Thiepval Memorial to the Missing. His younger brother, Frank, also enlisted, joining the 5th (Reserve) West Riding Battalion in November 1914. He was to survive the hostilities and is likely to be the same man who went on to be the landlord of the George Inn at Upper Denby with his wife, Mabel from 1930 to 1958.

Willie Wilcock (1896–1917)

Private. No. 240989. 2/5th Battalion Duke of Wellington's Regiment. Willie was born in the Halifax area to Harry Wilcock (a steelworker) and Mary Ann Womersley. By 1901 he was living in the household of William Wormald (a platelayer on the Penistone railway) at Revel Bottom in Denby Dale. William employed a housekeeper, Emma Womersley, a widow with three sons who all lived-in, and the sister of Willie's mother. We can only assume that Mary Ann had died between Willie's birth in 1896 and the census returns of 1901 and that William Wormald was content to house five children at his home, none of whom were his. By 1911, Willie's sister Ethel was also living here working as a twister, Willie was a plush finisher, both at a local mill. Willie was killed in action at the Battle of Bullecourt on 31 May 1917. He has no known grave but is commemorated on the Arras Memorial to the Missing. His effects were sent back to Ethel, who had by this time married to Oliver Burgess (at Gawber in 1914), the couple living at Higham near Barnsley.

Joseph Womersley (1895–1917)

Private. No. 245310. 10th Battalion Durham Light Infantry. He was born in Leeds, the son of Alfred and Alice Womersley, later of 4 St Pauls Street, Huddersfield. He lived at Denby Dale and was employed by J. Kitson & Sons, brickworks, in the village. He enlisted in December 1914 and was reported missing, presumed killed on 16 October 1917 aged 21. He has no known grave but is commemorated on the Tyne Cot Memorial to the Missing.

Hildred Woodhouse (1896–1915)

Private. No. 13559. 10th Battalion Duke of Wellington's Regiment. Born at Almondbury the son of Arthur Woodhouse, landlord of the Commercial Inn at Cumberworth and his wife Mary Ellen. He was employed by Hollingworth's contractors of Cumberworth and was also a member of the choir at St Nicholas's church in the village. He enlisted in September 1914 and embarked for France in April 1915. He died from injuries sustained on 4 November 1915 when his dugout collapsed, he was 19. He is buried in the Royal Irish Rifles Graveyard, Laventie, France.

Frank Wray (1899–1918)

Private. No. 58110. 5th Battalion King's Own Yorkshire Light Infantry. Formerly No. 7427 Duke of Wellington's Regiment. He was born at Cumberworth, the son of George Henry (a railway signalman) and Martha Wray, who moved to Dearne Terrace, Denby Dale, after her husband's death. Frank was killed in action on 2 September 1918, aged 19, and is buried at Vaulx Hill Cemetery, France.

Second World War

Walter G. Alexander

Details currently unknown.

Newell Ellis (1914–1940)

Sergeant. No. 1381160. Pilot, VR 160 Squadron. He was born in 1914 and lived at Norman Croft in 1940 with his mother, Bertha and worked as an elementary schoolmaster. He enlisted at Euston sometime after August 1940 and died on 15 January 1943. He is buried at Tripoli War Cemetery, Libya.

Roy Phillip Hargrave

Gunner. No. 14275646. Royal Artillery 79th Field Regiment. He was born in about 1924 to James B. and Elsie Hargrave of Leak Hall Crescent, Denby Dale, and was brother to Sheila. He died on 15 May 1944 aged 20. He is buried at Cumberworth.

John Hirst (1915–1943)

Lance Corporal. No. S/200802. Royal Army Service Corps. He died on 2 December 1943 aged 28 and is buried at Bari War Cemetery, Italy. He was the husband of Agnes Hirst of Denby Dale.

Selwyn Horn (1926–1947)

Gunner. No. 14137006. 46 Lt AA Regiment Royal Artillery. He died on 18 September 1947 aged 21. He was the son of Frank and Henrietta Horn of Lower Cumberworth. The Cumberworth parish register notes that there was no church ceremony when he was buried. We can only assume that Selwyn was badly injured during hostilities and died some time after the war had ended.

Alfred Horsley (1914–1941)

Mechanician 1st Class. No. D/KX82489. Royal Navy – HMS *Repulse*. Alfred died on 10 December 1941, aged 27, when the *Repulse* was sunk by the Japanese:

> The first attack began at 11:13 when 250 kilogram bombs were dropped from eight G3Ms from an altitude of 11,500 feet. The battle-cruiser was straddled by two bombs, then hit by a third which penetrated through the hangar to explode on the armoured deck below. This inflicted a number of casualties and damaged the ship's Supermarine Walrus seaplane, which was then pushed over the side to remove a fire hazard.
>
> Anti-aircraft fire damaged five of the Japanese bombers, two so badly that they immediately returned to Saigon. In the ensuing attacks, *Repulse* was skilfully handled by her captain, Bill Tennant, who managed to avoid 19 torpedoes as well as the remaining bombs from the G3Ms. However, Repulse was then caught by a synchronised pincer attack by 17 Mitsubishi G4M torpedo bombers and hit by four or five torpedoes in rapid succession. The gunners on the *Repulse* shot down two planes and heavily damaged eight more, but the torpedo damage proved fatal. At 12:23, Repulse listed severely to port and quickly capsized with the loss of 508 officers and men. The destroyers Electra and Vampire rescued the survivors, including Captain Tennant.

Alfred is commemorated at Plymouth Naval Memorial. He was the son of Herbert and Agnes Horsley and the husband of Lillian Horsley of Denby Dale.

Donald Mudd (1915–1943)

Flight Sergeant. No. 1017561. Air Gunner, Royal Air Force Volunteer Reserve. He died on 16 October 1943, aged 28, and is buried at Cawthorne Cemetery. He was the son of Charles Richard and Mabel Mudd of Oakfield Cottage, Denby Dale and husband of Ida E. Fish of Denby Dale, who he married in 1941. In 1939 Donald was recorded to be working as a wages clerk.

Frank Winston Peace (1923–1945)

Flight Sergeant. No. 1622410. Wireless Operator and Air Gunner, Royal Air Force Volunteer Reserve 221 Squadron. He died 8 March 1945 aged 21 and is buried at Rhodes War Cemetery, Greece. He was the son of Haydn H. Peace and Isabel Roebuck of Brentwood, Cumberworth. Haydn was a tailor's cutter in 1939 and Frank was a tailor's apprentice in the same year.

John Desmond Schofield (1917–1941)

Ordinary Telegraphist. No. P/JX201963. Royal Navy, HMS *Vanessa*. He died on 20 June 1941 aged 24. He was the son of Henry and Maria Schofield of Denby Dale and was recorded as a journeyman optician in 1939. John died of wounds inflicted when the *Vanessa* was attacked, the damage report continues:

> Vanessa 19 June 1941. One direct hit 100kg action fused bomb. While escorting a convoy off Cromer (the *Vanessa*) was attacked by an enemy aircraft. A direct hit was sustained at the fore end of No. 1 boiler room and the bomb finally burst on the ships bottom in No. 1 boiler room. The outer bottom was blown upwards over the length of No. 1 boiler room and 9ft. forward of it, between 2nd longitudinal starboard and bilge keel port and a hole 6ft. by 9ft. was made in the outer bottom. Severe damage was caused to the surrounding structure. The upper deck plating was split and blown upwards from near the after end of No. 2 boiler room to the bulkhead at the fore end of No. 2 oil fuel tank and the E.R.As and C.P.Os messes. Immediate flooding of No. 1 and 2 boiler rooms and No. 2 oil fuel tank took place. No. 1 boiler room was wrecked, No. 1 boiler exploded and No. 2 boiler was severely damaged. The forward funnel was blown overboard and the after funnel was wrecked.

John did make it off the ship and back to England, but he died at the Royal Navy sick quarters in Great Yarmouth.

Ivor Haydn Shobbrook (1915–1945)

Corporal. No. 7520279. Royal Army Medical Corps. He was born in Bedwelty, Monmouthshire (around fifteen miles North of Cardiff) on 5 March 1915, to George Shobbrook and Winifred Daniels. By 1936 the family were living at Hemsworth, Barnsley, both Ivor and his father earning their livings as coal hewers until at least 1939. In April 1941 Ivor married Phyllis Horn (a worsted textile mender), the daughter of Herbert Horn and Mary Hutchinson who ran the Crown Inn at Birdsedge from at least 1936. By now, Ivor was a member of 225 Parachute Field Ambulance in the Medical Corps. He was wounded on 18 July 1944 and died 24 March 1945 aged 30 and buried at Reichswald Forest War Cemetery, Germany. He is recorded on the War Memorial in Grimethorpe, though it is interesting to note that the Denby Dale War Memorial misspelt his surname as Shodbrook. As Ivor and Phyllis were married during the war they never had a chance to settle in their own home before Ivor was killed, and Phyllis can be found living with her parents, still at the Crown, in 1947, it is possible they remained here until the pub closed down in the 1960s.

The Crown Inn, Birdsedge, circa 1900.

Gilbert Stringer (1914–1941)

Grave of Gilbert Stringer at Upper Denby
churchyard.

Gunner. No. 11268100. Royal Artillery. Gilbert was born in 1914, the
only child of Jos and Rosetta Stringer. Jos and Rosetta Creighton were
married at Scissett in July 1907, Jos was recorded to be the son of Joshua
Stringer (a labourer) living at Clayton West and employed as a miner.
Rosetta was the daughter of Joseph Creighton, a hawker. Jos and Rosetta
can be found in 1911 living at Kitchenroyd with the Creighton family. Jos
in this case is likely to be the shortened form of Joshua in which case we
can find Jos and his family living at Squarefold, Clayton West in 1901:

Name	Age	Occupation
Joshua Stringer	56	General Labourer
Harriet Stringer	53	
Joshua Stringer (Jos)	22	Miner/Hewer
Fred Stringer	20	Miner/Hewer
Annie Stringer	18	Doffer in Mill
Willie Stringer	14	Doffer – Woollen Mill
Edith Stringer	12	Scholar

This family can be traced back to its origins in Birstall in 1494, before they moved on to Almondbury, Kirkburton and Shelley, finally landing in Clayton West with the above mentioned Joshua, who was born at Shelley in 1845 and died at Clayton West in 1913.

Rosetta Stringer died in 1922 when Gilbert was only 8 years old and Jos remarried a Denby Dale girl, Ada Spivey, in April 1925. Ada was the daughter of John William Spivey and Sarah Avison. The family can be found living at Polygon Terrace in Denby Dale in 1881, prior to moving onto High Street (today's Wakefield Road) by 1891. By 1911 they were at Fearn Lee House in the village. In 1901 Ada was working as a general domestic servant, while two of her sisters, Helliaria and Tryphena, worked in the textile industry. The family moved to Springbank, Denby Dale, and it was here that Jos Stringer died in 1936; he is buried at Upper Denby. We next encounter Ada and Gilbert in 1939, just prior to the onset of Second World War. They are still at Springbank with Ada recorded as undertaking unpaid domestic duties and Gilbert as a rayon

Upper Cumberworth church, circa 1900.

warp healder. Gilbert joined up shortly after the war began, though we know nothing other than that he was a Technical Battery Gunner in the Royal Artillery. He died on 26 October 1941, aged 27, at Holmecroft, Louth, Lincolnshire, of bronchopneumonia and emphysema, his death was registered the following day when the death certificate records Ada as his stepmother. His body was returned home and buried with his father in the family plot at Upper Denby. Ada continued to live alone at Springbank until she too passed away on 9 October 1954; she is buried with Jos and Gilbert at Upper Denby.

The Soldiers of Birdsedge in the
First World War

Edwin Allott 1888–1948

Courtesy Birdsedge Village Hall.

Private. No. 36539. 1/6th Northumberland Fusiliers. Edwin was the son of Edward Allott (1851–1928) of High Flatts, and Clara Stenton (1850–1918). This branch of the Allott family originated at Silkstone and it was John Allott (1770–1850) and his wife, Martha Wood (1771–1857), who made the move to High Flatts in the latter part of the eighteenth century. Their son Edwin (1810–1870) and his wife Jane Beaumont (1815–1900) were the parents of Edward mentioned above. John Allott was recorded as a stonemason in 1841 and his son Edwin was recorded the same in 1851. The family trade continued with Edward, who was noted to be a stonemason in all the census returns from 1871 through to 1911, and his son Edwin, aged 22, was also a stonemason in the 1911 returns, as was his elder brother, Henry, most likely both in the employ of their father.

Edwin was one of at least seven children born to Edward and Clara, all at High Flatts, though a further detail regarding the whereabouts of their home is furnished in the 1881 census returns which record them at Strines, High Flatts. Edward, Clara and their children were all practising members of the High Flatts Quaker community. Edwin became a Private in the Northumberland Fusiliers and fought in France and Flanders. He was reported missing on 17 July 1918, but was later found to have been captured by German forces and was being kept as a prisoner of war in Germany. A final document dated 21 January 1919 records his release and that he was back in England. In 1939 we find Edwin living at Rockly House, High Flatts, but now married, to Edith (born 1889) and with a son, Fred (born 1916), the implication from this is that the couple were married during, or just prior to the outbreak of, the war. Edwin is noted to be a contractor/builder/mason and Fred was a mason/bricklayer continuing the family tradition. Edwin died at Rockly House on 19 June 1948 and is buried at the Friends Burial Ground, High Flatts.

George Bower (1896–1967)

Courtesy Birdsedge Village Hall.

Lance Corporal. Italian Expeditionary Force. George Bower had his roots in Barnsley with his grandfather, George Bower (1804–1883), who had married Mary Mellor (1840–1921) as his second wife. George initially hailed from Brampton, Derbyshire, and was an iron moulder. George and Mary had a large family which included daughters: Sarah, Elizabeth Ann, Mary Ann and Jane. Their elder brother was Henry, who was born at Park Bridge, Ashton Under Lyme, but arrived in Barnsley when his parents moved here during the late 1870s. Henry (a coal miner) married Rose McHugh (1863–1901), and had at least six children, George was the fifth of these in November 1896. George was only around five years old when his mother died and was sent to live with his grandmother, Mary, at Crosspipes, Birdsedge, who had been a widow for thirteen years by the time George was born. The family can be found in the 1911 census where

Mary was noted to be 71 years old, the one remaining daughter, Jane (Janie) was 30, a cloth millworker, and George was now 14 and employed in a local textile mill. It is of interest to note that we have met Janie before in the section on Charles Godfrey Hinchliffe. Janie married his brother, Wilfred Stanley Hinchliffe, at the age of 37 at Queen Street Chapel, Huddersfield in 1918. Wilfred Stanley gave his occupation as Machine Gun Guards (MGG)Regiment in the register, residing at Burncote Farm, Gunthwaite. After the end of the war Wilfred Stanley and Janie went on to live and work on the farm with Janie's elder brother, William Bower, Janie died in 1963. Meanwhile, George Bower had joined up for the war effort; he would have been of age in November 1918 and he later became involved with the Italian Expeditionary Force. He saw out the war and returned home to continue working in the textile industry. In 1931 he married Beatrice Kenworthy at Shepley and the couple can be found in 1939 living at number 4, Ten Row, Birdsedge, George employed as a fettler/mill-hand.

Thomas Sykes Broadbent (1889–1962)

Courtesy Birdsedge Village Hall.

Private. No. 77229 & 35806. Northumberland Fusiliers. Thomas Sykes, known as Sykes, was the son of Henry Broadbent (1859–1922), a woollen and worsted weaver, and Hannah Sykes (1860–1945), who were married at Upper Denby in May 1885. He was the couple's youngest son and the family can be found living at Cross Pipes, Birdsedge, in the 1891 census, including Sykes's elder brothers Norris Sykes (aged 9) and Verdi (aged 4). It is apparent that Hannah was determined to keep alive her family name in that two of her sons bore it. We could also perhaps surmise that the musical compositions of Guiseppe Verdi might have been responsible for the other. By 1911 the family were noted to be living at Park Head Row, Birdsedge; Norris has by now gone his own way, but Verdi and Sykes had followed their father and become fancy worsted power loom weavers. Sykes initially joined up for the war with the 1st West Yorkshire Regiment

(No. 50369), he was next a part of the 2nd Yorkshire and Lancashire Regiment (No. 52893), before finishing up with the Northumberland Fusiliers. On one of his enlistment forms there is a note explaining that he was once rejected as unfit to enter the armed forces on account of his buck teeth. Sykes saw out the conflict and returned home to his wife, Lillian Kaye (1891–1973) and young son Jack, born in 1915 after he was demobbed. By 1939 we can find the family living on Commercial Road, Skelmanthorpe, Sykes was working as a joiner at a local colliery while Jack was a power loom weaver, also with the household was Sykes's mother Hannah, who was by now in her late seventies and recorded as being incapacitated. War returned this year and Jack Broadbent joined up for the cause as an infantryman with the Duke of Wellington's (West Riding) regiment in 1939. He saw action in France and Belgium but was not evacuated at Dunkirk as this operation ceased on 4 June, he was killed in action on 11 June and buried at De La Seine-Maritime, Haute-Normandie, France. Sykes and Lillian continued to live on Commercial Road until at least 1945, Sykes passing away in 1962.

Verdi Broadbent (1887–1958)

Courtesy Birdsedge Village Hall.

Private. No. 47023. Durham Light Infantry. As noted above, Verdi was the elder brother of Sykes Broadbent. We have already noted him in various records and that he worked as a fancy power loom weaver prior to the war; in fact, in 1901, aged only 14, he had worked as a woollen feeder in one of the local mills. On 21 November 1914 at the High Street Chapel in Huddersfield, Verdi was married to Hypatia Hey, both aged 27 and both working as plush weavers. Verdi was noted to be living at the family home at Park Head, Birdsedge, and Hypatia at Smithy Lane, Skelmanthorpe, her father being George Hey, a plush weaver. Hypatia is yet another unusual name in this book; she was named after the female Hellenistic Neoplatonist philosopher, astronomer, and mathematician, who lived in Alexandria, Egypt, then part of the Eastern Roman Empire from 355 to 415BC approximately. Hypatia was a prominent thinker of the Neoplatonic school in Alexandria where she taught philosophy and astronomy. Verdi signed up for the war effort, initially with the West Yorkshire Regiment (No. 75762) and then with the Durham Light Infantry (No. 47023). He, like his brother, made it through the hostilities and returned home to his family. In 1939 he can be found living on Station Road, Skelmanthorpe with Hypatia, working as a woollen worsted weaver, he died in 1958.

John Burley (1887– Unknown)

Courtesy Birdsedge Village Hall.

Air Mechanic 1st Class. No. 46315. Royal Air Force. John was born at Hoylandswaine to Charles Burley (1855–1925) and Sarah Jane Apperley (1855–1927) in 1887. We have already encountered this family as John's sister, Maude Minna Burley, married the Australian, Charles Ralph Douglas Bell, at Denby in 1917. I would refer the reader to that section of the book for more details of the Burley family. As for John, we can find him in 1911 living with his family at Denby (more than likely at High Flatts) working as a gardener at a brewery. By this time his father Charles was no longer a farmer of independent means and was working as a farm labourer. John's First World War Service seems to begin on 2 March 1916. He was initially posted to the Royal Naval Air Service/ Royal Flying Corps, Rank A, Mechanic 1, Driver – Military Transport. On 10 June 1918 he joined Number 20 Balloon Company (comprising Nos. 34 & 48 Balloon sections) and became a part of the 1st Balloon Wing. He was discharged from military service on 17 March 1919.

Fred Cartwright (1888–1953)

Courtesy Birdsedge Village Hall.

Private. No. 41972. 12th Manchester Regiment. Fred was the son of Jonas Cartwright (1856–1908) and Sarah Ann Woodhead (1856–1942). Jonas, originally from Hepworth was described as a stone delver/stone dresser at a quarry in various census returns. Sarah Ann was a native of Ingbirchworth where their first two children, Lucy (born 1880) and Beatrice Alice (1892–1972) were born. The family had moved to Park Head, Birdsedge by the time Fred was born in 1888 and he was followed by Percy (1890–1970) and Elsie (1893–1966). By 1901, Fred was 13 years old and working on a local farm as a cow boy, by 1911 (after his father's death) he had followed in his footsteps and become a stone dresser at a local quarry. Fred enlisted for the war and joined the 12th Manchester Regiment. A military communication on 1 June 1918 reported that he was missing. A further communication dated 26 September 1918 described that in a list received from the German government, he was a prisoner of war in Germany. He was released and back in England by 20 December 1918. Fred appears to have lived out the rest of his life in Birdsedge until his death in 1953.

Percy Cartwright (1890–1970)

Courtesy Birdsedge Village Hall.

Sapper. No. 108885. Royal Engineers – Special Brigade. Percy was the younger brother of Fred listed above. He was born in Birdsedge in 1890 to Jonas and Sarah Ann Cartwright. By 1911 he was working as a joiner's apprentice, a career he made a success of. He seems to have enlisted for the war in 1914 as a Sapper in the Royal Engineers. The term 'sapper' is derived from the French word *sappe* ('spadework', or 'trench') and became connected with military engineering during the seventeenth century, when attackers dug covered trenches to approach the walls of a besieged fort. They also tunnelled under those walls and then collapsed the tunnels, undermining them. These trenches and tunnels were called 'saps,' and their diggers came to be called 'sappers'. In modern armies, sappers serve three functions. They provide tactical support on the battlefield by installing portable bridges, tank traps, and other construction; they build major support facilities, such as airports, supply roads, fuel depots, and barracks; and they are assigned additional tasks, including the disarming and disposal of mines and unexploded bombs and shells and the preparation and distribution of maps. Sapper is the Engineers' equivalent of a Private. Percy survived the conflict and returned home where, on 5 July 1920, he married Emma North (1890–1986) at Netherfield Chapel, Thurlstone. From at least 1927 (and possibly earlier) Percy was the landlord of the New Inn public house at Upper Denby. He and Emma remained here until at least 1939 though, as was usual at the time, Percy continued to work as a joiner. Records show that Percy remained in Upper Denby throughout Second World War and lived locally until his death in 1970.

Thomas Kaye Chappel (1895–1955)

Courtesy Birdsedge Village Hall.

Private. No. 5183. Later: 241963. 1/7th Prince of Wales Own (West Yorkshire) Regiment. Thomas is recorded in the baptism register at Upper Cumberworth on 5 March 1899 where his mother is noted to be Martha, a single woman living at Birdsedge. It is possible that his father was named Kaye, as in his name, but there is no further evidence for this. Martha was the daughter of John James Chappel (born at Fulstone 1850–1894), a shoddy presser of Birdsedge and his first wife, Martha (1852–1873). She was born in 1873, a result of which may have been her mother's death. She can be found in the 1891 census returns living with her family at Spring Head House, Crosspipes, Birdsedge, working as a cloth finisher. In the same survey her father is noted to be a ground labourer at a local brewery. John James remarried in 1875 to Caroline Peace and had at least three further children, including Mary Hannah in 1877, to whom we will return. John James died in 1894 and we can next find young Thomas in the 1901 census living with his grandmother Caroline's family at Crosspipes with her two daughters, Emma Peace Chappel (a woollen twister) and Ada Chappel (a woollen weaver). We catch up with Thomas again in 1911 when he was living at Cumberworth with his aunt, Mary Hannah Chappel. Mary Hannah (born 1877) was the daughter of John James and Caroline Chappel and stepsister of Martha, the mother of Thomas. She had married Fred Nightingale, a stone quarry worker, and they had a daughter, Mary, who was a scholar in 1911. In this survey Thomas was recorded as a woollen piecer. It is possible that Thomas's mother Martha went on to marry Willie Noble in 1898 at Kirkheaton and lived at Dalton, passing away in 1926. Thomas enlisted for the war in 1915, aged 20, with the Prince of Wales Own (West Riding) Regiment, he listed his occupation to be a mill-hand on the form. After being demobbed he returned home and on 19 March 1921, was married at Lockwood to Amy Helme. Thomas was an engineer's labourer and living at 9 Forest Road, Dalton, Huddersfield, and Amy was a weaver of Lockwood, daughter of William Edward Helme, a painter. It is interesting to note that Thomas gave his grandfather's name as his father in the marriage register, even though he never knew him. In 1939, Thomas, aged 44, was living at 98 Greenhead Lane, Dalton, working as a woollen weaver, with Amy, aged 38, a worsted and woollen weaver and the couple's two children, Constance (born 1921) a shorthand typist, and Eric (born 1923), an apprentice constructural engineer. Thomas died in 1955 and is buried at All Hallows, Almondbury.

Percy Dalton (1884–1947)

Private. Seaforth Highlanders. Percy was born in Skelmanthorpe to George Henry Dalton (1859–1933) and Clara Haigh (1856–1937). George was originally from Silkstone, in 1901 was living near Toby Wood and a foreman at a brick-making company in Denby Dale. In later census returns he was noted to be a miner/collier, eventually moving to Nether End, Lower Denby. Clara was the daughter of Samuel Haigh of Ingbirchworth and the marriage took place at Upper Denby in 1878. After leaving school Percy became an apprentice tailor and we can find him thus in the 1911 census returns. His war service records are scanty to say the least, but one perhaps does allude to him. Dated 23 December 1918, it notes that 2nd Lieutenant P. Dalton, Seaforth Highlanders, Gordon Highlanders with WO329 Company was eligible for a war medal. Percy married Ellen Tyas in 1915 at Upper Denby where he describes himself as a tailor, apprenticeship complete. Ellen (1880–1959) was the daughter of Henry Tyas of Birdsedge, a shoemaker. The couple can be found in 1939 living at number 4, Ten Row, Birdsedge, Percy self employed as a tailor.

Willie Exley (1900–1972)

Courtesy Birdsedge Village Hall.

Private. King's Own Yorkshire Light Infantry. Willie was born in 1900 to Charles Exley (born 1869) and Caroline Ellis (born 1868). The family were at Fulstone in 1901 when Charles was recorded as a mason's labourer. By 1911 they were at Upper Cumberworth, though Caroline was by now a widow bringing up her three young children alone, Willie (aged 10) and Edith (aged 6) were both born at Fulstone, the youngest sibling, Hannah Eliza (aged 3) was born at Heator, Cumberworth. Willie would only have turned 18 years old in the final year of the war and records for him at this time are thin on the ground to say the least. He did return home unscathed and went on to marry Amy Evelyn Liles (1898–1976, known as Evelyn) at Denby church in 1925. The couple had two children, Edwin Peter (1927–1989) and Jacqueline Carol (1929–1980). In 1939 the family were living at Parkhead, Birdsedge, Willie listing his occupation as a stone planer.

Walter William Gathercole (1882–1960)

Courtesy Birdsedge Village Hall.

Gunner. No. 166679. Royal Field Artillery. Walter was born at Methwold, Norfolk the son of George Gathercole (1859–1935) and Mary Ann Risborough (1863–1926). He had four sisters, Elizabeth (born 1879), Alice Louisa (1888–1973), Mildred 'Millie' Kate (1893–1983), and Mabel (1897–1939). The family can be found living with Mary Ann's father William Risborough (a gardener) in 1891, when George was noted to be an agricultural labourer. After school, Walter followed his father and worked for local farmers, probably alongside him. In the meantime his elder sister Elizabeth had married Henry Nursey (also from Norfolk) but for reasons unknown they left East Anglia to live at High Flatts near Denby where they began a family. The 1911 census returns record their children as Harry, Connie, Verena and Robert, and also note that Walter had followed them North and was living with them. Henry

Nursey was a teamer at a local stone quarry and had found work for Walter as a stone cutter. A document dated 8 December 1915 informs us of Walter's enlistment for the war with the Royal Field Artillery, he has also changed occupation again and is now recorded as a dye works labourer, aged 33. He survived the hostilities and ended up marrying late in life, in 1938, to Nellie Butler (1893–1970) in Huddersfield, Walter was 56. In 1939 we can find the couple living on Heator Lane, Cumberworth, Walter working as a roadside quarrier, though by 1946 they had moved to Friezland Cottages in Shepley, he died in 1960.

John Benjamin Hargrave (1889–1957)

Courtesy Birdsedge Village Hall.

Private. No. 33533. Machine Gun Corps. Benjamin Hargrave was born at Denby in 1889, the son of Henry Hargrave (1848–1912) and Ellen Parker (born 1855 at Ingbirchworth). We can find Henry Hargrave in the 1881 census returns working as a farm servant for his father James (born 1820) at Gunthwaite. James was a farmer of 16 acres and a joiner, and so it was natural that his younger son, Dyson, was also employed by him as a joiner's assistant. By 1891 Henry had struck out on his own and was a farmer himself at Delph Hill Farm, on Upper Denby Common. In the census returns of that year he recorded that he was born at Kitchenroyd, Denby Dale. He had also married Ellen and begun a family with the birth of Ellen (1883), followed by Elizabeth (1885), Sarah (1887), James Benjamin (1889), Herbert (1893) and William Henry Dyson Hargrave in 1895. By 1901 the family had moved to Hunger Hill, Fulstone where

Henry continued as a farmer. Another move had taken place by 1903 when the family arrived in Birdsedge and baptised William Henry Dyson at Denby church, Henry's occupation was now listed to be a labourer. In 1911 the family were recorded at Ingbirchworth only a year before Henry died. Two of his sons, James Benjamin and William Henry Dyson, were employed as brick yard labourers. James Benjamin (known as Benjamin) enlisted for the war as a Private with the Machine Gun Corps. After being demobbed he returned home to marry Elsie Craven at Cumberworth on 2 August 1919, the couple moving to live at Wood Nook in Denby Dale. On the marriage book entry, Benjamin was noted to be living at High Flatts and Elsie at Denby Dale. The couple had a daughter, Sheila, in 1934 and by 1939 had completed their final move to Leak Hall Crescent, Denby Dale. A record from that year informs us that Benjamin was a general labourer though incapacitated. He died in 1957.

William Henry Dyson Hargrave (1895–1972)

Courtesy Birdsedge Village Hall.

Private. No. 241132. 1/5th West Yorkshire Regiment. William Henry Dyson (known as Dyson) was the younger brother of the above Benjamin. He had a similar upbringing to his brother and even worked at the same brick yard as a labourer. He enlisted with the West Yorkshire Regiment and saw out the conflict to its conclusion. Soon after his return home he married Amy Fryer (1900–1954) in 1920 in Huddersfield and a daughter, Freda, was born in 1921. By 1939 the family was living at Linthwaite where Dyson was employed as a woollen teaser and Amy as a woollen weaver. Dyson died in 1972.

Albert Haywood (1894–1967)

Courtesy Birdsedge Village Hall.

Private. No.49734. 1/9th King's Liverpool Regiment. Albert was the son of Willie Haywood (1864–1918) and Selina Senior (1866–1908), the couple were married at Cumberworth in 1890 where Willie was noted to be a labourer. Willie was the son of Richard Haywood and the wonderfully named Jet Holden, whom he married in 1861. Richard was born at Denby but lived at Crosspipes, Birdsedge. In 1861 he was recorded as a 'slubber' in the marriage entry, this involved removing the imperfections, or 'slubs', in the yarn prior to spinning. By 1871 he is listed as a woollen miller, but by 1911 he is a labourer. In 1891 Willie was recorded as a stone labourer and in 1911 as a quarry stone cutter. Willie and Selina had at least seven children: Beatrice Alice (1891–1957), George Willie (1892–1926), Albert, Norman (1897–1963), Lily (1899–1901), Fred (1901–1970) and Selina (1906–1988). Albert enlisted for the war with the King's Liverpool Regiment, he was wounded in action in France but recovered and was discharged from service on 29 November 1918. He married in 1931 at New Mill to Amy Maude where he gave his occupation as a woollen teaser and his abode as Park Head, Birdsedge. The couple had a daughter, Sheila M. Haywood in 1933, and in 1939 were living at New Row, Ingbirchworth. Albert died in 1967 and Amy in 1975.

Norman Haywood (1897–1963)

Courtesy Birdsedge Village Hall.

Private. No. 66084. Machine Gun Corps. Norman was the younger brother of the above named Albert Haywood. He enlisted with the Machine Gun Corps and saw action in Mesopotamia. This campaign was fought in the Middle East with troops from Britain, Australia, New Zealand and British India against the Ottoman Army (Turkish, Arab, Kurdish and other forces) in Egypt, Palestine, Arabia, Mesopotamia (Iraq) and Persia (Iran). Of all these battles, the Allies' defeat at Gallipoli (Turkey) is best remembered due to the losses incurred by the Allies. Norman returned home and married Harriet Ann Hey at Cumberworth in 1935 where his occupation was given as a brewer's drayman, Harriet was a twister in a textile mill. In 1939 we find the couple living at Kirkhouses, Cumberworth. Norman died in 1963.

Herman Douglas Heppenstall (1897–1979)

Courtesy Birdsedge Village Hall.

Guardsman. No. 19645. Coldstream Guards. Herman's family stretches back into the eighteenth century in their association with Upper Denby and High Flatts. James Heppenstall (1784–1862) was born at Maythorne near Leyburn in the Yorkshire Dales, but had arrived in Denby by 1841 when he and his family were living at Delph House and he was employed as a delpher in the quarry at Mosley Roughs run by George Norton. He married Martha Green and two of their sons also became involved with the quarry. Jonathan (born 1833) was a labourer at the quarry in 1851. James (1838–1890) was originally a delpher, though later he was a stone dresser. James became acquainted with George Norton's daughter, Elizabeth, and they were married at Denby church in 1864, he was 26, she was 20. Neither of them were literate and so both signed X by their names. There is more information on the Norton family and quarry in the appendices in this book. James had died prior to the quarry being abandoned in 1893 when George Norton died but his son, Benjamin (1866–1935), known and recorded as Ben, carried on the family trade. He was recorded as an above ground labourer in 1881, but by 1891 was a stone dresser, most likely at Denby Delf for George Norton his grandfather. The 1901 and 1911 census returns record him as a stone quarry man in one of the other local works. Ben married Sarah Ellen Dearnley (1867–1934) and had four children, all at the family home at High Flatts, Herman Douglas was the youngest of these. Known as Douglas, we can find him in the census of 1911, living at High Flatts with his family and working (aged 13) as a reacher-in on power looms at a woollen cloth mill. He signed up for the war effort and joined the Coldstream Guards, returning home after being demobbed at the end of hostilities. He married Helen Sophia Rushworth in 1923 at Shepley, where he gave his occupation as a cloth presser. In 1939, after the birth of two children, the family are recorded at 2 Field Cottages, Birdsedge, and Douglas was still employed in the textile industry as a woollen and worsted weaver. Douglas died in 1979.

All-in-One Tree of Herman Douglas Heppenstall

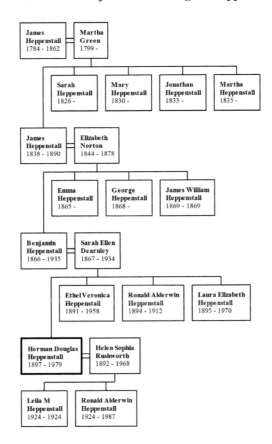

James Benjamin Heywood (1898–1955)

Courtesy Birdsedge Village Hall.

John Benjamin Heywood.

Corporal. No. 67270. Machine Gun Corps. James was the son of Robert and Mary Eliza Heywood, he was born at Shepley, one of at least seven children, but the family had moved to Birdsedge by 1899 as his younger brother, Herbert, and all the subsequent children were born here. Robert worked as a teamer (horses) for a brewery. After serving in France with the Machine Gun Corps, James married twice, firstly to Marion Webster (1905–1947) of Linthwaite, and secondly to Annie Gibson (1897–1955).

John Benjamin Heywood.

Annie Gibson, who married James Benjamin Heywood.

John Thomas Horn (1899–1987)

Courtesy Birdsedge Village Hall.

Private. No. 62533. King's Own Yorkshire Light Infantry. There were a large number of families bearing this name living in the Denby Dale and Cumberworth area, but this one begins in Stockport with John Horn who was born there in 1795 (died 1864). He met and married Sarah Kilner at Penistone in 1815 and had a son, Samuel (1816–1907), in Denby Dale. Samuel worked in the textile industry, as a wool dyer among other things, though by 1891 he was listing himself as a delpher and clothier on the census returns. He married Martha Lockwood in 1839, again at Penistone, though the family home for many years was at New Brighton, Birdsedge. They had at least ten children, the youngest of whom was Herbert William Horn (1871–1920). Herbert William married Emma Murgatroyd (1874–1941) in 1898 and their children were born in and around Birdsedge, though the family home was on Birdsedge Hill. Herbert

Herbert William Horn, father of John Thomas.

Annie Thorpe who married John Thomas Horn in 1925.

William had a varied career, in 1891 he was silk plush finisher, in 1899 a mechanic, in 1911 an engine tenter at a worsted cloth manufacturers and in 1925, a motor driver. An engine tenter oversaw the operation of the steam engine which drove the other factory machinery. They had six children, four boys and two girls. John Thomas arrived in 1899 and was only 15 years old when the war began. He did enlist but probably not before 1917 and his eighteenth birthday, as this was the lower limit for soldiers to join up. He joined the King's Own Yorkshire Light Infantry and we can find

Emma Murgatroyd (1874–1941) wife of Herbert William Horn and mother of John Thomas.

him on 1 July 1918 complaining of pyrexia of unknown origin. Pyrexia symptoms included raised body temperature and a fever, causes of which include infections such as colds and stomach bugs among other things.

He was sent to the sick convoy on 4 July then to the 2/2nd West Riding Ambulance, then to No. 36 Ambulance Train. He recovered and indeed was not demobbed until 22 November 1919. He returned home just in time to see his father before his untimely death in 1920, he is buried at Denby. John Thomas married Annie Thorpe at Denby in 1925 and had two children, Hazel and Derek. In 1939 we find him and Annie living at Kirkburton when John Thomas was working as a woollen warper, though he and Annie had the sideline of a grocers shop on Abbey Street. John Thomas died in 1987.

George Lockwood Horn (1898–1973)

Courtesy Birdsedge Village Hall.

Guardsman. No. 112195. Royal Garrison Artillery, Grenadier Guards. George was the brother of the above mentioned John Thomas Horn. George joined the Grenadier Guards during the war, enlisting when he was 18 years and 8 months old in 1916, when he listed his occupation as a cloth warehouseman. After being demobbed he married Clara Annie Wingrove (1897–1937) and had a son, Herbert William (1922–1985) at High Flatts. Clara's early death saw George remarry, to Edith Jones (1906–1988), and two further children followed, Clive (1940–2005) and Winstan (1941–1990). In 1939, George was recorded as living at High Flatts and working as a joiner for a works maintenance department.

George Edwin Liles (1893–1962)

Courtesy Birdsedge Village Hall.

Private. No. 212419. Royal Field Artillery. George Edwin was the son of Frank Liles (1871–1947) and Ida Horn (1871–1935). Frank was born in Hunshelf but for much of his life was a farmer at Green Gates Farm, Ingbirchworth. He and Ida had at least twelve children, the majority of whom were baptised on 25 July 1905 (St James's Day), which must have been an interminably long ceremony. Frank eventually moved on to Green Lane Farm, High Flatts, where he can be found in 1939. George Edwin can be found in the 1911 census returns as a labourer at a local pipe works.

Norman Ernest Liles (1899–1947)

Courtesy Birdsedge Village Hall.

Private. No. 44842. East Yorkshire Regiment. Norman was the brother of George Edwin mentioned above. Norman saw out the war and emigrated to Australia in 1922. He boarded the ship *Berrima* (a P&O Branch Service) on 28 December bound for Melbourne, aged 23, when he described himself as a farmer of High Flatts. Records suggest that he married a woman named Blanche and had a family in Australia. It is just possible that he had a cricket ground named after him. A Norman Ernest Liles was a founder member of the Redhead Cricket Club in the Lake Macquarie/Newcastle area of New South Wales. In the 1940s he worked to build the ground later known as the Liles Oval and also took on a coaching role. He died while umpiring a match in 1947.

Joseph Lindley (1891–1947)

Courtesy Birdsedge Village Hall.

Private. Machine Gun Corps. Joseph, known as Joe, was born at 81 Wentworth Road, Blacker Hill, Worsborough, to Joseph Lindley (1865–1923) and Eliza Ann Howard (1867–1910). Joseph (the elder) was a miner all his life. The couple had five children, Joseph, Maude (1892–1952), Albert Edward (1894–1929), Tom (1897–1950) and James (born 1900). We find Joe (the younger) in the 1911 census returns, aged 20, and working as a rope lad at an underground colliery. He joined the Machine Gun Corps and it was on one of his periods of leave from the army that he was married. The ceremony took place on 20 October 1917 at Upper Denby church, Joe was 26 and described as a Private Soldier. His bride, Jane Elizabeth Thorpe, was 20 and from Birdsedge. After being demobbed at the end of hostilities Joe returned to Birdsedge where we can find him in 1939, living with Jane at 3 Ten Row in the village and working as a kiln firer at a local pipe works. Joe died in 1947.

Joe Thomas Marsden (1891–1970)

Courtesy Birdsedge Village Hall.

Gunner. No. 117658. Royal Garrison Artillery. This particular branch of the Marsden family originated in Ingbirchworth. John Marsden (1766–1848) was a farmer there and he and his wife, Mary Moorhouse (1767–1842) had a family which included Alfred Marsden (1811–1872). Alfred was recorded variously in the census returns as weaver (1841), hand loom worsted weaver (1851) and cotton worsted weaver (1861). He married Ann Senior (1821–1888) and had a son, Thomas Marsden (1843–1909) at Ingbirchworth. By 1861, Thomas was a cotton worsted weaver like his father. In 1873 he married Hannah Travis at Upper Denby church when he listed his occupation to be a labourer, and by 1871 he was an excavator. Things had changed for the better by 1881 when he and his family were living at Lower Longroyd, Cumberworth, and Thomas was a farmer of ten acres and a weaver. By 1901 he was farming at Greenhouse Farm,

Carr Hill Road, Upper Cumberworth, but his death in 1909 saw most of his family leave here. The 1901 census returns illustrate the family:

Thomas Marsden	58	Head	Farmer
Hannah Marsden	53	Wife	
Martha Elizabeth (Lee)	25	Daughter. Widow.	Alpaca weaver
Harriet Ann	23	Daughter	
Mary Jane	20	Daughter	Alpaca weaver
Ellen	16	Daughter	Worsted piecer
Hannah	14	Daughter	Worsted piecer
Joe Thomas	9	Son	Scholar
George Thomas Marsden Lee	2	grandson	

The 1911 returns explain what went on. Thomas's daughter, Mary Jane, was married soon after to Lewis Dearnley (farmer and painter), who took over Greenhouse Farm and while their young family was growing up, Joe Thomas Marsden lived and worked here as well.

Joe Thomas enlisted for the war with the Royal Garrison Artillery and became part of 308 Siege Battery. He survived the conflict, indeed he was still on active duty in July 1919 when he was mentioned in despatches, it was also recorded that he was now a part of the 57th Siege Battery. He eventually returned home and married a woman whom at present I know only as Hilda. They can be found living at Birdsedge in 1939, when Joe gave his occupation as a stone sawer. They were still here in 1948. Joe died in 1970.

Mitchell Mellor (1888–1972)

Courtesy Birdsedge Village Hall.

Sapper. No. 262013 & WR28761. Royal Engineers Quarry Company. Mitchell was the son of John (born 1849) and Clara (born 1854) Mellor who ran the Junction Inn at Wooldale, John was also a quarryman. Mitchell married Annie Jepson (1889–1987) in 1913, who was born at Denby but living with her family at Birdsedge at the time of the wedding, which took place at Christ Church, New Mill. Her father, William (1855–1906), had been a domestic servant coachman in 1891 living at High Flatts but by 1901 was a farmer, an occupation also given on the marriage certificate. Mitchell seems to have followed his father into quarrying and stonemasonry, a skill he was to put to good use during the war. He joined the Royal Engineers as a sapper, later becoming a part of the Roads and Quarry Company WO329. He would have been involved in digging the trenches at the front lines of the Allied armies. Mitchell and Annie had a son, Douglas, in 1917, and in 1939 can be found living at Kirkburton, Mitchell employed as a stonemason and Douglas as a mechanical engineer. Mitchell died in 1972.

Ben Mitchell (1895–1982)

Courtesy Birdsedge Village Hall.

Private. No. 313624. Tank Corps. We begin our look at the Mitchell family with Ira Mitchell (1835–1899), who lived and farmed at Thurlstone. He was born at Langsett and ended up being the farmer at Moor Royd Farm (64 acres). He married twice, initially to Charlotte Shaw (1839–1870) at Penistone in 1860, she bore five children, including William, to whom we shall return. Her early death saw Ira remarry, this time to Ann Biltcliff (1847–1911), and a further eight children were born. When Ira died he left £1,405 5s in his will to be split between his widow, Ann, his son William from his first marriage, and his son Charles Ernest from his second marriage. William Mitchell (1860–1922) began his working life, naturally, on the farm with his father from at least 1881 to 1891, but by 1901 he had become a carter for a brick and tile company. In 1892 he married Mary Elizabeth Womersley at Northumberland Street Chapel,

Huddersfield, the couple living variously at Ingbirchworth, Crow Edge and Cumberworth. By 1901 they were at Pottergate, Fulstone. A return to the farming life soon took place and in 1911 we find the family living and working at Pog Hall Farm, High Flatts as the census returns illustrate:

William Mitchell	50	Farmer	Thurlstone
Mary Elizabeth Mitchell	45		Thurlstone
Edith Mitchell	18	Worsted weaver	Ingbirchworth
Ben Mitchell	15	Sanitary pipe labourer	Thurlstone
Sam Mitchell	13	Sanitary pipe labourer	Cumberworth
Annie Mitchell	10	school	Thurlstone
Amy Mitchell	5		Denby
Lucy Mitchell	3		Denby

William (Billy) Mitchell with his wife, Mary Elizabeth and daughter Edith in about 1894.

Mary Elizabeth Mitchell, nee Womersley who married William (Billy) Mitchell in 1922.

All of William and Mary's children were baptised at Crow Edge Wesleyan Methodist Chapel.

As we can see, Ben and Sam Mitchell both worked for a local sanitary pipe manufacturer, probably either Naylor's or Kitson's works in Denby Dale. Ben noted himself to be a labourer on his enlistment form for the war and that he was 20 years and 8 months old. He was initially posted to the 4th Reserve Cavalry but ended up being a soldier in the Tank Corps. He survived the conflict and went on to marry Gertie Kippax (1896–1985), the sister of his brother Sam's wife, Mary. The couple had two children, Donald and Joan, and can be found in 1939 living at High Flatts; Ben was a farm labourer and his son was a bottle filler in a brewery. Ben died in 1982 at Burton Cottages, Penistone Road, High Flatts.

Pog Hall Farm, High Flatts, circa 1970.

Sam Mitchell (1897–1985)

Courtesy Birdsedge Village Hall.

Sam Mitchell and Mary, his wife.

Private. No. 66090. Machine Gun Corps. As we have seen above, Sam was the younger brother of Ben. He enlisted for the war with the Machine Gun Corps. Once demobbed, he returned home and married Mary Kippax, the sister of Gertie, who had married his brother Ben. The Kippax sisters were the daughters of Joshua Marsden Kippax (a confectioner and yeast dealer) and his wife Ellen of The Bank, Thurlstone. The couple had a son, Douglas, in 1923 and we can find the family in 1939 living at Lane Head, Kirkburton; Sam working as a farmer in his own right, though Douglas, now aged 16, was a brewery bottle filler. Sam died in 1978.

John Henry Mosley (1896–1967)

Courtesy Birdsedge Village Hall.   Ellen Tinker who married John Henry
Mosley in 1920.

Rifleman. No. 7557 (or 7554). 18th King's Royal Rifles. John Henry was the son of Fred Mosley (1862–1901) and Emma Conway (1874–1955) of Town End, Shelley. Fred had been a mill hand, but by 1901 he was working as a market gardener. After Fred died in 1901 the family moved to Wakefield Road, Denby Dale where, in 1911, we can find John Henry and his brother Ernest both working as domestic gardeners. John Henry joined the King's Royal Rifles and a report dated 24 October 1916 lists him as wounded, he was in fact discharged from service on 26 December 1916, probably due to this injury. In 1920, John Henry married Ellen Tinker (1896–1977) at Cumberworth church, she was the daughter of Harris Tinker, a one-time barrel man and the couple had a daughter, Gladys, in 1922. Ellen was the sister of two other Birdsedge serviceman included in this book, Friend and Jim Tinker. In 1939 the family was living on Penistone Road, Birdsedge, and John Henry is noted to be disabled (probably the injury sustained in battle), but still operating as a general labourer and motor driver. He died in 1967.

Beardsall Thorpe (1897–1954)

Courtesy Birdsedge Village Hall.

Private. No. 31137. Duke of Wellington's Regiment. Indian Expeditionary Force. Beardsall was one of seven children born to Albert Edward Thorpe (1864–1932) and Ann Matthews (1869–1918). The family had strong connections with Fulstone, Shepley and Birdsedge. Albert Edward's father Uriah and his wife Mary can be found living at Hirst Buildings, Birdsedge in 1881. Uriah was a coachman/groom, though all of his offspring were employed in the textile industry except Albert Edward who, at 13 years old, was still a scholar. Albert married Ann Matthews at Denby church in 1890 where his father is described as a groom living at Birdsedge, Ann's father was Seth, a spinner living at Shepley. They initially lived at Fulstone, Albert working at a stone quarry. Their children followed soon afterwards: Uriah (1890–1950), Haydn (born 1891), Jane Elizabeth (1893–1972), George Beardsall (1896–1897), Phoebe (1896–1979), Beardsall (1897–1954) and Friend (1902–1974). The 1901 census returns record the family living in the Sovereign area, and in 1911 at Shepley. Beardsall was born at Shepley in 1897 and joined the war effort in 1914 at the minimum age of 18. The Birdsedge roll of honour informs us that he was a part of the Duke of Wellington's Regiment and played a part during hostilities in India. He returned home after being demobbed and found employment as a mental nurse, possibly at the nearby Storthes Hall which was founded as a mental asylum in 1904. He married Elsie Mary Metcalfe (1897–1996) at Shelley church in 1927, he was noted to be living at Rose Cottage, Birdsedge, at the time, but by 1939 the couple had moved to Kirkburton (perhaps to be nearer Beardsall's place of work). He died in 1954 and was outlived by his wife by forty-two years.

Friend Tinker (1895–1930)

Courtesy Birdsedge Village Hall.

Gunner. No. 2322. Royal Field Artillery. Friend was the son of Harris Tinker (1865–1935) and Ann Eliza Dyson (1861–1936). Harris was born at Fulstone, the son of James Tinker, once a publican but also a cloth weaver, and spent his working life as a general labourer. Ann Eliza was born at Bolsterstone but was living at Cumberworth when the couple married at Cumberworth in 1894. Her father, George, was employed as a miner. Harris had moved around the area: in 1871 he was at Cross Pipes, Birdsedge, with his family, before a move to Ten Row in the village by 1881, when we find Harris working as a mill piecer and joined by a much younger sister, Elizabeth (Lizzie) in 1877. By 1891 his father had become the landlord of the Sovereign Inn, Shepley, and so the family were living here, Harris recorded as being an assistant in public house. After his marriage Harris and Ann Eliza are next recorded as living at Rockhouse, Cumberworth. Their family began with Friend Tinker in 1895 and he was followed by: Ellen (1896–1977), Kate (1897–1978), Jim (1900–1995), Cora (1901–1993) and Kenneth (1905–1983). By 1911 the family were

Harris Tinker and his wife, Ann Eliza, parents of Jim and Friend Tinker.

living at Fairleigh Cottage, Cumberworth though it is interesting to note that Harris was now employed as a 45-year-old brewer's labourer. Two of his elder daughters were also of working age, Ellen had become a mill hand spinner and Kate a mill hand doffer. The eldest son had flown the nest by now and Friend can be found recorded as a cow boy on farm, in the census of 1911, working for James Lodge at Toby Wood Farm, Denby Dale. The Lodge family were also notable horse breeders, indeed, James's elder son, Joseph, was noted to be a horse man on the same survey. Friend Tinker enlisted for active service on 1 June 1915 and joined the Yorkshire and Lancashire Regiment as a Gunner. It was while he was on leave the

Left to right: Ada and Friend Tinker, with his sister, Kate and her husband George Welburn.

following year that he got married, on 18 October 1916, at Cumberworth to Ada Higgs (1892–1972) who produced a son, Denis (1918–2007) soon afterwards. In the marriage register Friend recorded his occupation as Gunner Royal Field Artillery. Friend returned home from the war and can still be found in Birdsedge in 1926, but moved on soon afterwards to East Retford where his death was recorded in April 1930 at a tragically young age. Harris Tinker died in 1935 and is buried at Cumberworth; his wife, Ann Eliza passed away the following year.

Jim Tinker (1900–1995)

Courtesy Birdsedge Village Hall.

Private. West Yorkshire Regiment. Jim was the younger brother of the above named Friend Tinker. He was still a scholar in 1911 living with parents Harris and Ann Eliza at Fairleigh Cottage, Cumberworth. He followed his brother into the field of battle enlisting with the West Yorkshire Regiment on 7 February 1918. This was the final year of the war, it ended nine months after Jim began his basic training but he had obviously got a taste for the life. After he was demobbed he can soon be found re-enlisting on 26 February 1919 at Catterick when he joined the Seaforth Highlanders, but his military career was not destined to be a long one, on 19 December 1919 at Fort George, Ardersier, Inverness-shire he was discharged on medical grounds as being unfit for war service. He returned home and soon afterwards was married at Cumberworth church to Bertha Gibson (1901–1996) on 3 June 1922. Jim was by now employed as a mill-hand, Bertha was from Birdsedge, the daughter of George Edward Gibson, a coachman. A son, Charles Eric (1924–1995) was to follow. Jim was still working in the Huddersfield area in 1939 as a woollen loom tuner but as he grew older he decided to retire to the East Coast, where his death is recorded in Bridlington in 1995.

Arthur Tyas (1882–1962)

Private. No. SE/21231. Army Veterinary Corps. Arthur was the son of Henry Tyas (1851–1921) and Eliza Biltcliff (1847–1916). Henry was a cordwainer, a man who made new shoes rather than a cobbler, who only repaired older shoes. He took after his father, Mathias Tyas (1825–1876), who lived and worked in Upper Denby. By 1881 Henry and Eliza were living at Birdsedge, indeed, in the 1891 census returns they are described as living at 'old Birdsedge'. Their children were all born here; Ann (1879–1902), Ellen (1881–1959), Arthur (1882–1962) and Alice (1885–1925). Henry continued to ply his trade up until his death and also taught his only son, Arthur, to follow in his footsteps. His second daughter,

All-in-One Tree of Arthur Tyas

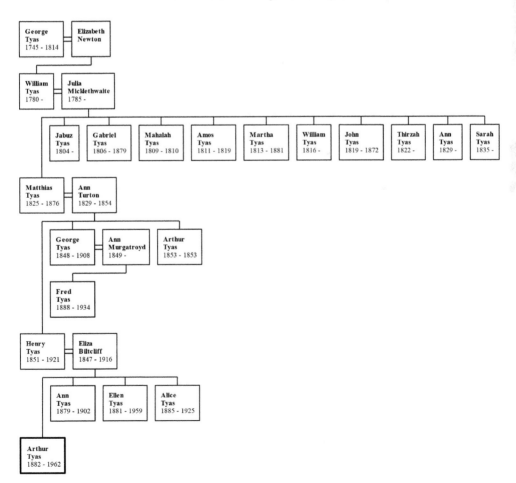

Ellen, became a tailoress. Arthur joined the Army Veterinary Corps and survived the conflict to return home. He married Edith Hannah Woodhead in 1924 though she died only three years later. He remarried to Annie Garner (1898–1969) in 1928 and had three children, Mavis, Mabel and Margaret Wendy. Arthur seems to have lived his whole life in Birdsedge until his death in 1962.

Rowland George Welburn (1899–1966)

Courtesy Birdsedge Village Hall.

Private later Corporal. No. 5/3815 later 75314. Duke of Wellington's West Riding Regiment. Later Northumberland Fusiliers. Rowland was the son of George Arthur Welburn (1869–1944) and Caroline Bullimore (1873–1942). George was born in Beverley and was a farm labourer/teamsman. The family can be found in 1911 living at the Carr, Shepley, but later moved to Fairlea Farm, Birdsedge. Rowland was initially a soldier in the West Riding Regiment but later became a part of the Northumberland Fusiliers. A report dated 17 July 1918 recorded that he was missing in action during the war, but a further report dated 3 December 1918 noted that he was released from a PoW camp in Germany and now back in England. In 1922 he married Kate Tinker (1897–1978, daughter of Harris Tinker whom we have met before in this book). Rowland was recorded as a 'fetler' of Crosspipes, Birdsedge. The couple went on to have a son, Jack Bullimore Welburn (1924–1999). In 1939 they were living at Park Head, Birdsedge and were still there in 1945.

Driver George W Haywood (Royal Field Artillery). Courtesy Birdsedge Village Hall.

Private Arnold Rhodes (Princess of Wales – Yorkshire Regiment). Courtesy Birdsedge Village Hall.

Sergeant Jack Robinson (1/7th West Riding Regiment. Courtesy Birdsedge Village Hall.

Arthur Senior (Durham Light Infantry). Courtesy Birdsedge Village Hall.

Memorial Tablet for the Fallen of Birdsedge. Courtesy Birdsedge Village Hall.

Private Percy Robinson (Labour Corps) is also mentioned on the War Memorial inside Birdsedge Village Hall.

Birdsedge Roll of Honour
Second World War

Birdsedge & District

Roll of Honour 1939–1945
Killed in Action – 24 March 1945 – Corporal I.H. Shobbrook RAMC
(6th Airborne)

Private – F. Allot	Lance Corporal – C. Moorhouse
Stoker – I.E. Armitage	Sergeant – G. Moorhouse
Sergeant – C. Bramall	Staff Sergeant – (AC) – H. Mosley
Lance Corporal – E. Briggs	Able Seaman – G.T. Neagle
Driver – C. Brook	Captain – H.S. Netherwood MC
Driver – F. Dearnley	Flight Sergeant – W.J. Netherwood
Lance Corporal – H. Dearnley	Cadet Petty Officer – C. Parker
Lance Corporal – G. Dickinson	Flight Sergeant – J. Robertshaw
Corporal – G. Earnshaw	Wing Commander – C. Roebuck
Lance Bombadier – P. England	Leading Aircraftsman – W. Smith
Signaller – R. Fretwell	Leading Aircraftsman – J. Taylor
Sapper – T. Hirst	Driver – F. Thorpe
Leading Aircraftsman – Harry Horn	Driver – F. Whitehead
Leading Aircraftsman – Herbert Horn	Private – H.A. Wibley
Leading Aircraftsman – W. Horn	Private – J. Wilde
Private – B.L. Lindley	Guardsman – A. Wright
Corporal – W. Littlewood	Sister – C. Allot
Corporal – H. Lockwood	Private – F. Lee
Corporal – D. Mitchell	Private – G. Moorhouse
Gunner – N. Mitchell	

Appendix 1

The Norton Family, quarry owners at Denby Delf

Earlier in this book we encountered Edwin and Herbert Norton Jackson and discovered that Herbert bore the middle name after his mother's maiden name: Martha Ann Norton. In research undertaken prior to this work I investigated the stone quarry known as Denby Delf, now the beauty spot Mosley Roughs; its life as a sand-stone quarry and its owners through time. This is the story of Martha Ann's father, George Norton, not to be confused with the Scissett mill owner of the same name.

On the Denby Enclosure Award Map dated 1802, some of the land at Denby Delf was owned by William Bosville, a member of the land owning family at Gunthwaite, though he was largely based in London. Because of the changes in field boundaries it is difficult to tell exactly if the Delf belonged to Bosville alone. His land was to the immediate East of Madras House (then known as Bombay) and was abutted by that of Hannah Littlewood, then Wheetman Dickinson, Sir Charles Kent and Mrs Varelst and Dickinson & Littlewood. As the Enclosure Award Map was produced to show who owned which parcels of land, it only mentions a few buildings such as the Chapel, but it is of interest to note that 'Slate Delf' quarry was recorded to the west of the Penistone Turnpike Road as part of a huge swathe of land owned by The Honourable Richard Lumley Savile. This delf is sited upon the same spot as the later 'Rusby Delf' and is almost certainly one and the same; ergo, this is where we find the Rusby family quarrying. There is nothing on the map to suggest a quarry at Denby Delf at this time.

William Bosville was described as 'a celebrated bon vivant'. He was schooled at Harrow and entered the Coldstream Guards in 1761. He served with a regiment for part of the American War and travelled widely on the Continent. At home he lived in London where he entertained guests at his house in Welbeck Street at exactly five o'clock every weekday.

He did not involve himself in his Yorkshire estates and was eccentric in his manners, always dressing in the manner of a courtier of George III. He was an ardent supporter of the reform party of the Whigs and was friendly with Horne Tooke and William Cobbett. When William Bosville died at the end of 1813, the male line of Bosville of Gunthwaite became extinct and the main beneficiary of his will was his nephew, Godfrey, the second son of Elizabeth Diana Bosville and her husband Alexander Macdonald.

Land close to that of William Bosville's was being farmed by Joshua Mosley; this is very likely where the term 'Mosley Roughs' comes from and probably has its origins in the eighteenth century. Joshua Mosley may have held land further up the lane prior to Enclosure, explaining the gap between his lands and the Delf. At this time all the land around the Delf was in private ownership, and the lane known today as Denby Common was, in 1802, called the Huddersfield Road.

Quarry Owner's & Merchants of Denby

(as listed in the Trade Directories of the Nineteenth Century)

Piggot's Directory 1834
James Rusby (merchant in stone)

Whites Directory 1838
John Ellis (High Flatts – stonemason & Quarry Owner)

Whites Directory 1857/8
George Norton (Stone Merchant)

Whites Directory 1866
George Norton (High Flatts – Stone Mason & Quarry Owner)
Charles Rusby (Quarry Owner)
Ben Ellis (High Flatts – Quarry Owner)
John Micklethwaite (Quarry Owner)
John Moore (Quarry Owner)
James Moore (Quarry Owner)

Whites Directory 1870

John Micklethwaite (Upper Denby – Quarry Owner)
George Norton (High Flatts – Quarry Owner)

Kelly's Directory 1901

Burton Rusby (farmer Delf House)
   No further quarrying activities are mentioned from this point onwards, including directories for 1912, 1922 and 1936.

Ordnance Survey Map of 1845.

A sandstone quarry is mentioned at Denby Delf on the Ordnance Survey Map of 1845 and a further nearby one is marked as Moor Royd sandstone quarry. It is of note that Rusby Delf is also marked to the North West of Delf House Farm. Another sandstone quarry is marked at Falledge to the southwest of the farm.

As we can see, there is a concentration of quarries in the area between High Flatts and Upper Denby.

George Norton was born in 1817 at Denby to John Norton and Mary Beever. George would have been 28 in 1845, when we know for a fact that the quarry was operating. In the 1841 census he was noted to be living at Moor Royd (which could have been classed as High Flatts) with his mother and father and remaining family members, and was described as a stone miner, as was his father John (now aged 65). A brother, Benjamin aged 20, was a 'delpher'. A delpher, or delver, was someone who worked in a stone quarry. A delver is anyone whose work involves digging, and may include coal-miners and quarry-workers.

George married Martha Hepenstall and had a family of at least eight children. By the time of the birth of their son Daniel in 1848 George was noted to be a quarryman/labourer living at Pog Hall Farm, High Flatts. By 1851 we can find George and Martha living at Pog Hall with Martha's father, Daniel Hepenstall, who was a farmer and stone merchant, George at this time was a labourer in a stone quarry. Daniel Hepenstall died in 1852 aged 55, and it seems that George was able to take over both farming and quarrying activities as the sitting tenant.

We have seen that the nineteenth century trade directories list George Norton as a stonemason/quarry owner in 1857/8, 1866 and 1870. By the time of the 1861 census he is recorded as a farmer of 37 acres and quarry owner employing five men and two boys. His son, James, is recorded as a carter, so he may well have been working for his father; Daniel Norton, George's younger brother was also an employee as a stone delver at the quarry as well as a lodger with the family at Pog Hall. George's daughter, Elizabeth, worked as a dairy maid on the farm.

In the 1871 census, George was described as a farmer of 36 acres and a sandstone quarry merchant. His son, Daniel, aged 23 (labourer quarryman) and brother, Daniel, were still working at the quarry, though his brother died in 1876 aged 41, George was by now 54.

An estate sale (on behalf of the Bosvilles) advertised in the *Sheffield Daily Telegraph* dated Saturday 6 March 1875, is the proof that it was at the quarry at Denby Delf that George Norton was operating:

Sales by Mr A.E. Wilby.
Highflatts and Birdsedge, in the Township of Denby,...
Valuable freehold family residence, farms, dwelling-houses, land and stone quarry. To be sold at auction by Mr Arthur E. Wilby, at the house of Mr Sykes, the Rose and Crown Hotel, in Penistone, on Thursday, the 18th day of March, 1875, at three o'clock in the afternoon (unless previously disposed of by private contract, of which due notice will be given), and subject to such conditions as will then be produced.

(includes)...
Lot 6. All that quarry of Superior Stone known as 'Denby Delf Stone' (similar in quality to the far-famed Green Moor Stone situate near to Lot 4), and now in the occupation of and worked by Mr. George Norton.

And the several closes of land adjoining thereto, in the occupation of the late Mr Seth Dalton's representatives, viz.,

Lot No. 30. Quarry Field, and above-mentioned Quarry therein: 5 acres, 0 roods, 36 perches.

Lot No. 31 Near Quarry Field: 2 acres,1 rood,11 perches.

Lot No. 32. Far Quarry Field: 2 acres, 1 rood, 35 perches.

Total (more or less): 10 acres, 0 roods, 2 perches.

The Quarry and one acre of the stone adjoining thereto in the close called the Quarry Field are in lease to Mr George Norton for the term of 20 years, from the 1st of March, 1873, at a minimum yearly rent of £60 for 240 yards of stone (surface measure) and 5 shillings a yard for all above that quantity.

This lot will be sold subject to the above lease, and the covenants, conditions, and agreements therein contained.

This lot well deserves the attention of stone merchants, builders, &c.: it adjoins the highway, late the Huddersfield and Penistone Turnpike road, and is within a short distance from the Penistone, Shepley, and Denby Railway Stations respectively.

NB: Lot 4 in the sale related to four closes of land adjoining Denby Lane, in the occupation of Dalerever Burdett, comprising Low Common, Upper Low Common, Far Low Common, Near Low Common, which is the area on the other side of the road.

From the records it would seem that most of this land was bought by Walter Norton of Rockwood House, Denby Dale, a member of the highly successful Scissett mill-owning family.

As we have seen, there were a number of quarries operating at this time in Denby and High Flatts so we cannot be sure of the employer in the following newspaper report regarding a Denby quarryman, though it is possible he worked at Denby Delf for George Norton:

Barnsley Chronicle 13 Sept 1879.

Attempted suicide at Denby.
John Gaunt, quarryman, Upper Denby, was placed in the dock, and Inspector Wade stated that on the 26th August he was found in Swift Wood, Upper Denby, bleeding profusely from wounds to his arms, as already published in our columns.—P.C. Thistlethwaite gave evidence as to finding Gaunt.—In answer to the Bench, Gaunt said didn't know why he attempted to injure himself. He had apparently been recovering from the effects of a drinking bout at the time he committed the deed.—After promising never to do anything of the

kind again he was handed over to PC Thistlethwaite to be conveyed to the custody of his friends.

In the 1881 census George is listed as a farmer of 45 acres, employing two labourers and one boy and a sandstone quarry merchant employing two labourers and one boy. By 1891, George was 74 years old and had moved to Laithe House, High Flatts, though he was still recorded as a farmer and stone merchant. His eldest son, James, played a major role as quarryman in his father's business, and he was by now married to Harriet Turton with a son, Arthur.

George Norton died in 1893 and his wife in 1894 and with him, it would seem that the family's quarrying business at Denby Delf was wound up, the lease for the quarry had expired in March 1893. James Norton can be found at Pog Hall Farm in 1901 working as a farmer and employer, though by 1911, he and Harriet were living at a two room house on Denby Common and he was employed as a carrier; he died in 1919. George's second son Daniel was a stone carrier/delver during the time he and his wife, Sophia, were having some of their children, this is the period from 1873–1882, after this he is again listed as a carter, confirming the family's departure from quarrying; he eventually moved to Lockwood, Huddersfield before his death in 1914.

To summarise: The quarry at Denby Delf appears to have been founded between 1802 and 1841 on land owned by William Bosville, Lord of the Manor of Gunthwaite. The Norton family living at Moor Royd and later Pog Hall Farm, almost adjacent to the site, became farmers and quarrymen taking over both from Daniel Hepenstall in 1852. Daniel may have originally rented the site from the Bosvilles. In the 1870s the Bosvilles sold their land to Walter Norton and this appears to have included Denby Delf quarry. By 1893 (a period of say around forty years), the quarrying seems to have been abandoned and there are no further mentions of any quarrying activity at Denby up until the 1930s. By the 1960s the quarry was being used as a tip for broken gravestones from the church and so was totally abandoned by this time.

All-in-One Tree of Martha Ann Norton

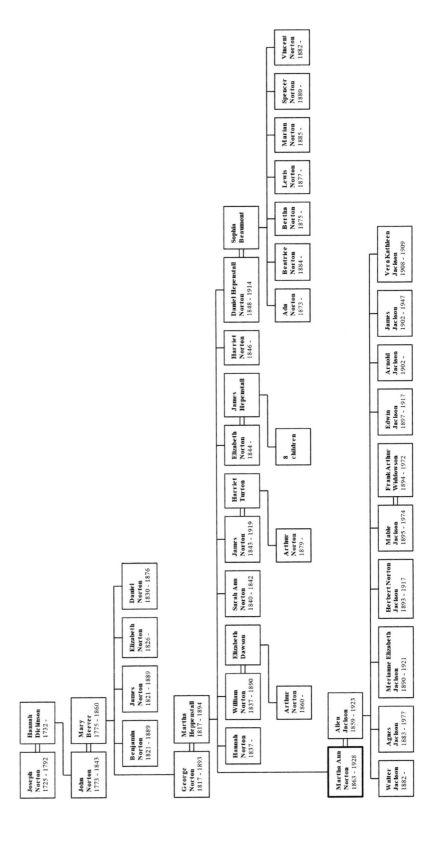

Particulars and Plans

OF

VALUABLE FREEHOLD & TITHE-FREE

ESTATES

SITUATE AT

HIGH FLATTS AND BIRDSEDGE,

IN THE TOWNSHIP OF DENBY, IN THE PARISH OF PENISTONE,

AND

DEARN,

IN THE TOWNSHIP OF FULSTONE, IN THE PARISH OF KIRKBURTON, IN THE COUNTY
OF YORK,

TO BE SOLD BY AUCTION,

BY

MR. A. E. WILBY,

AT THE ROSE & CROWN HOTEL, IN PENISTONE, IN THE COUNTY OF YORK,

ON

THURSDAY, THE 18th DAY OF MARCH, 1875,

At THREE O'CLOCK in the Afternoon (unless previously disposed of by Private Contract, of which due
notice will be given), and subject to such Conditions as will be then produced.

The Tenants will show the respective Lots, and Plans and all further particulars
may be obtained of Mr. JOHN GREAVES, Land Agent, Thurlstone, near Penistone;
Mr. JOHN WOOD, Land Agent, Newhouse, Denby Dale, near Huddersfield; the
AUCTIONEER, at his Office at Denby Dale aforesaid; Mr. FREDERICK A. BINNEY,
Solicitor, 22, St. Ann's Square, Manchester; or of

DRANSFIELD & SONS,

SOLICITORS,

PENISTONE.

Cover page of the land sale document of 1875.

PARTICULARS.

LOT 1.

All that substantial stone-built Family Residence, called "MILL BANK HOUSE," situate at High Flatts aforesaid, with the Garden in front, and the Barn, Stables, Cowhouse, Workshops, and other Buildings adjacent thereto (No. 1 on Plan).

Also all that COTTAGE and Garden, near to the last described premises (No. 2 on Plan).

And also the several Closes or Parcels of LAND following, namely :—

No. ON PLAN.	DESCRIPTION.	QUANTITY.		
		A.	R.	P.
3	House Close or Kitchen Croft, including the Road thereto from High Flatts Lane	1	3	0
4	Long Croft	1	1	25
5	Square Field	1	3	10
6	Mill Field	2	1	4
7	Croft	0	0	23
8	Site of old Windmill, and Yard thereto	0	0	24
9	Would or Acre Close	1	0	14
10	High or Kiln Field	2	1	26
11	High or Middle Mill Field	1	3	29
12	High Field or Laith Croft	1	2	33
13	Bank	1	3	21
14	Plantation	1	0	0
15	Bank Ing	1	3	8
16	Quarry Piece (not enclosed)	0	1	17
17	Drive and Plantations adjoining	0	1	20
	Total (more or less) including sites of Buildings, &c.	A21	0	31

The House and Premises comprising this Lot were lately and until his death the residence and in the occupation of Herbert Camm Dickinson, Esq. (the late owner thereof), but are now in the occupation of the Vendors and Mr. John Goacher.

This Estate is suitable for a Gentleman's Residence, or the House might at little cost be converted into an Educational Establishment, for which (being in a healthy and bracing situation, and within a convenient distance of Huddersfield, Sheffield, Barnsley, Wakefield, and other Towns), it is well adapted.

LOT 2.

All that stone-built Dwelling-house, called "THE MIDDLE HOUSE," situate at High Flatts aforesaid, with the Gardens and vacant Land in front, and the Outbuildings and vacant Land at the back thereof (No. 18 on Plan), now in the occupation of the representatives of Miss Wright, deceased, and the Outbuildings and large Garden, called "THE LOW GARDEN" (No. 19 on Plan), near thereto, now in the occupation of the Vendors.

Also those three COTTAGES, situate to the West of the above described Dwelling-house, with the Gardens, and vacant Land thereto belonging (No. 20 on Plan), one of which Cottages is in the occupation of G. H. Rusby, and the others are unoccupied.

And also those three Closes of LAND, lying near the above premises, and in the occupation of Mr. G. W. Moxon, namely :—

No. on Plan.						A.	R.	P.
21	Round Flatt	....	....	....	....	....	4	3	8
22	Ley Close	....	....	....	....	....	3	1	1
23	Low Ing and Shrog	....	....	....	....	....	4	0	10
	Total (more or less) including sites of Buildings, &c.				....	A12	3	8

The Dwelling-house and Outbuildings in this Lot might, if required, be at little cost converted into a convenient Farm Homestead.

Attention is called to the Spring, and also to the never-failing Stream of Water in the Land part of this Lot, which Water might be made available for the supply of the populous district of Denby Dale, or for any Manufacturing or other purposes.

N.B.—The Purchaser of this Lot is not to have any right of road over any part of Lot 1.

LOT 3.

All that DWELLING-HOUSE, situate at High Flatts aforesaid, with the Yard adjoining (No. 24 on Plan), and the Close of LAND, called the "Tan Yard Close," near thereto (No. 25 on Plan), the site whereof contains 3A. 0R. 25P. (more or less).

It is believed the Land contains the same valuable Bed of Stone as that now in work in the Moor Royd Quarry near thereto.

Lots 1 to 3 listed in the 1875 land sale document.

3

LOT 4.

All those four Closes of LAND, situate near to Lot 3, and adjoining on the North to Denby Lane, and in the occupation of Dalarever Burdett, namely :—

No. on Plan.						A.	R.	P.
26	Low Common	....	....	....	....	2	0	8
27	Upper Low Common	....	....	....	....	3	1	38
28	Far Low Common	....	....	....	....	2	1	2
29	Near Low Common	....	....	....	....	2	1	9
	Total (more or less)	....	....	....	....	A10	0	17

LOT 5.

All that QUARRY of superior Stone, known as "Denby Delph Stone" (similar in quality to the far-famed Green Moor Stone), situate near to Lot 4, and now in the occupation of and worked by Mr. George Norton.

And also the several Closes of LAND adjoining thereto, in the occupation of the late Mr. Seth Dalton's representatives, namely :—

No. on Plan.					A.	R.	P.
30	Quarry Field and above-mentioned Quarry therein	....	....	5	0	36
31	Near Quarry Field	....	....	....	2	1	11
32	Far Quarry Field	....	....	....	2	1	35
	Total (more or less)...	....	....	....	A10	0	2

N.B.—The Quarry and one Acre of the Stone adjoining thereto, in the Close called "The Quarry Field," are in Lease to Mr. George Norton, for the term of 29 years from the 1st of March, 1873, at a minimum yearly rent of £60 for 240 yards of stone (surface measure), and 3s. a yard for all above that quantity.

This Lot will be sold subject to the above Lease and the covenants, conditions and agreements therein contained.

The whole of this Lot is believed to contain the same Beds of Stone as those now in work as aforesaid therein, and the whole of the Stone may be got by one or several Quarries.

This Lot well deserves the attention of Stone Merchants, Builders, &c.

It adjoins the Highway, late the Huddersfield and Penistone Turnpike Road, and is within a short distance from the Penistone, Shepley, and Denby Dale Railway Stations respectively.

LOT 6.

All those two Closes of LAND, situate at High Flatts aforesaid, adjoining on the South to Green Lane, and in the occupation of George Beaumont, namely :—

No. on Plan.						A.	R.	P.
33	Low Wilkinson Field	....	....	....	....	2	1	8
34	Far Wilkinson Field	....	....	....	....	2	1	8
	Total (more or less)....	....	....	....	....	A4	2	16

LOT 7.

All those two Closes of LAND, adjoining on the South to Lot 5, and on the North to Wind Mill Lane, and in the occupation of George Beaumont, namely :—

No. on Plan.						A.	R.	P.
35	Wilkinson Field	....	....	....	....	2	0	8
36	Near Wilkinson Field	....	....	....	....	2	1	8
	Total (more or less)....	....	....	....	....	4	1	16

LOT 8.

All those eight stone-built COTTAGES, called "Pump Street," fronting the Road (late Turnpike) at High Flatts aforesaid, with the Outbuildings and vacant Land thereto belonging (No. 37 on Plan), now in the several occupations of William Beaumont, George Beaumont, and George Norton and his under-tenants.

Also all those three other COTTAGES, called "Charles Street," with the Outbuildings thereto (No. 38 on Plan), and in the several occupations of George Norton and his under-tenants.

And also all those four Closes of LAND, adjoining and at the back of the above described Cottages, and now in the several occupations of John Goacher and Francis William Horn, namely :—

No. on Plan.						A.	R.	P.
39	First East Field	....	....	....	....	2	1	11
40	Second East Field	....	....	....	....	2	0	2
41	Third East Field	....	....	....	....	1	3	18
42	Fourth East Field	....	....	....	....	1	3	2
	Total (more or less) including site of Buildings	....	....	A8	1	8

The Land is of superior quality, well fenced, in a good state of cultivation, and believed to contain a valuable Bed of Building Stone.

The three last described Cottages might be converted into a comfortable Farm Homestead.

The attention of Millowners in the locality is called to this Lot, the Cottages being near to and convenient for the residence of their workmen.

LOT 9.

All that Farm House formerly called, "BIRDSEDGE," but now, "THREAD MILL HOUSE," situate at Birdsedge aforesaid, with the Barn, Stable, Cowhouse, and Outbuildings thereto belonging (No. 43 on Plan).

And also all those several CLOSES or PARCELS OF LAND therewith occupied, namely:—

No. on Plan.								A.	R.	P.
44	Burdett Field	....	....	....	....	....	....	3	2	20
45	Croft	....	....	....	....	....	....	0	3	5
46	Lower Far Rape Field	....	....	....	....	....	....	2	3	15
47	Upper Far Rape Field	....	....	....	....	....	....	2	2	7
48	Upper Near Rape Field	....	....	....	....	....	....	2	0	14
49	Near Lower Rape Field	....	....	....	....	....	....	2	3	25
50	Plantation	....	....	....	....	....	....	1	3	2
51	Upper West Field	....	....	....	....	....	....	2	1	31
52	Lower West Field	....	....	....	....	....	....	2	1	33
53	Fourth North Field and Fifth North Field, now in one	....	....	....	....	....	....	2	3	4
54	Plantation	....	....	....	....	....	....	1	2	6
55	Third North Field or Well Close	....	....	....	....	....	....	1	3	23
56	Second North Field	....	....	....	....	....	....	2	1	32
57	First North Field	....	....	....	....	....	....	2	2	21
58	First South Field	....	....	....	....	....	....	2	1	0
59	Second South Field	....	....	....	....	....	....	2	0	20
60	Third South Field	....	....	....	....	....	....	1	2	37
61	Fourth South Field	....	....	....	....	....	....	1	2	6
62	Fifth South Field	....	....	....	....	....	....	1	1	14

Total (more or less) including site of Buildings, &c.   A. 42   0   11

This Lot is in the occupation of Francis William Horn. It lies contiguous to the Road late the Huddersfield and Penistone Turnpike Road. The Buildings are in good repair, and same and the Land well supplied with water.

LOT 10.

All that stone-built Farm House, called "DEARN HOUSE," situate near High Flatts, but in the Township of Fulstone aforesaid, and abutting on the south to Wind Mill Lane, with the Barn, Stable, Cowhouse, Outbuildings, and Appurtenances thereto belonging.(No. 63 on Plan).

And also all those NINE CLOSES OF LAND thereto adjoining and therewith occupied, namely:—

No on Plan.								A.	R.	P.
64	House Field	....	....	....	....	....	....	5	0	0
65	Quarry Piece	....	....	....	....	....	....	5	0	8
66	Upper Far Ten Acres	....	....	....	....	....	....	10	0	26
67	Middle Ten Acres	....	....	....	....	....	....	10	0	4
68	Barn Field	....	....	....	....	....	....	9	1	16
69	Plantation or Fallow Field	....	....	....	....	....	....	5	0	4
70	Middle Five Acres	....	....	....	....	....	....	5	0	4
71	Near Five Acres	....	....	....	....	....	....	5	0	0
72	Lower Five Acres	....	....	....	....	....	....	5	0	10

TOTAL (more or less), including site of Buildings   A. 60   2   2

This Lot is in the occupation of George Day.

All the Lots are Freehold and Tithe Free, well Fenced, and Roaded, and believed to contain Beds of Building and other Stone.

Lots 1 and 2 are likewise believed to contain Coal.

The whole of the Lots are situate within a few miles of the Shepley, Denby Dale and Penistone Railway Stations respectively.

Lots 9 to 10 listed in the 1875 land sale document.

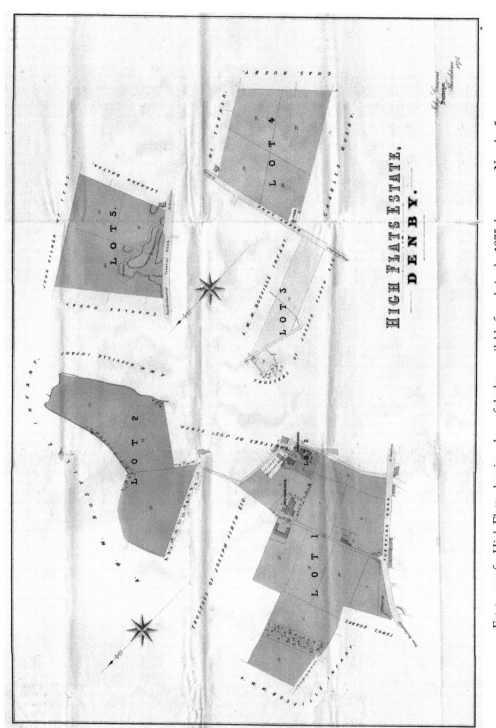

Estate map for High Flatts showing plans of the lots available for sale in the 1875 document. Note lot 5.

Appendix 2

Notes from Penistone Almanac

November 1942

Corporal Walter D. Heath, Royal Tank Corps, of High Street, Denby Dale, reported a prisoner of war in Italian hands. He had been missing since 20 June 1942. He served in France, Dunkirk and the Middle East and was wounded near Tobruk. He has a brother and a sister in the forces.

February 1945

Petty Officer George Bower of Highfield Farm, Denby Dale met his cousin, Sub Lieutenant John Leach of Clitheroe out in Ceylon.

Denby Dale taken from half way up Miller Hill, looking on to Victoria Terrace and Leak Hall, circa 1910.

May 1945

Petty Officer John Horsley, Royal Navy, of the White Hart Hotel, Denby Dale awarded DSM.

Guardsman Harold Burdett of Inkerman Cottages, Denby Dale arrived home after fifteen months as a prisoner of war.

Two Denby Dale brothers, Jack and Fred K. Fisher of Leak Hall Crescent, arrived home after being prisoners of war since St Valery in June 1940.

Trooper John W Thorpe of Low Field House, Denby Dale, arrived home after being taken prisoner of war at Tobruk in 1942.

Prisoner Norman Laundon (28) of Sykehouse, Denby Dale, taken prisoner at Boulogne in May 1940 arrived home.

Appendix 3

Evelyn & Bessie Heath and the Dickinson Family

The Dickinson family originated from the Kirkburton area with John Dickinson, who was born circa 1575/80. He had a son, another Henry, in 1635 who lived at Sheephouse, Penistone; he also became one of the first practising Quakers in the district and attended the Friends Meeting House at High Flatts. Henry was followed by his son, Daniel, also a Quaker, and he in turn by yet another Henry (1710–1786), who actually settled at High Flatts, close to the meeting house with his wife, Hannah Brook and their family. His son, Joshua (1755–1806) married Sarah Clark, remaining a Quaker at High Flatts and had at least seven children including Edward (1794–1868), who moved the short distance to Ingbirchworth to live. He was noted to be a hand loom weaver in 1851 and a cotton worsted weaver in 1861. His son, Joseph (1837–1874) remained at Ingbirchworth and was noted to be a cotton worsted weaver in 1861 and a fancy weaver in 1871. He was followed by his son, John (1857–1907), who married Elizabeth Hanwell and had at least eleven children, all at Ingbirchworth. John was a steel works labourer from 1881 through to 1901, but by 1891 (and probably till his death in 1907) he was also the licensed victualler of the Travellers Inn & Druids Tavern on the main road in Ingbirchworth. One of John's daughters, Harriet (1889–1963), went on to marry the Upper Denby joiner and undertaker, Joe Willie Heath, and had six children, including Evelyn and Bessie who were involved in Second World War. The family lived at the old Wesleyan Chapel in Upper Denby, a short distance from the age-old family joiner's shop, now demolished and replaced with a new house.

The Dickinson family were not only prominent at the early foundation of the Quaker movement, indeed, two family members associated with Birdsedge went on to become pioneers in industry. Both were named Elihu, one was known as the tanner and the other the clothier who

founded Birdsedge Mill. We have to go back to the time of Henry Dickinson (1600–1667), whose son Henry (1635–1719) was responsible for the line we have followed. Henry's brother, John (1636–1682), was the ancestor of the two more well known Elihu and I have included a little of their family history on the following chart, but for a much more in-depth history of this side of the family I would refer those interested to the work produced in *Denby & District II*.

Gravestone of John Dickinson and Elizabeth Hanwell at Upper Denby.

Evelyn and Bessie Heath, taken during the Second World War.

All-in-One Tree of Bessie Heath

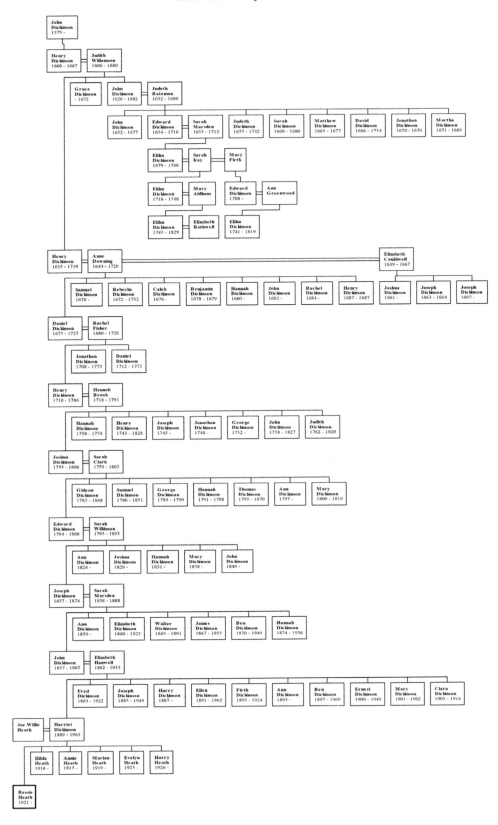